An Insider's Guide to Music City USA!

Nashville inside Out

Susan Chappell

Susan Chappell

TWO LANE PRESS, INC.

Also by Susan Chappell:
Day Trips From Nashville

First printing April 1996

ISBN: 1-878686-26-7

Printed in the United States of America

Text and cover design: Jim Langford
Map: Leigh Melton Singleton, *Nashville Banner* illustrator
Editing: Jane Doyle Guthrie

10 9 8 7 6 5 4 3 2 1   96 97 98 99 00

Two Lane Press, Inc.
4245 Walnut Street
Kansas City, MO 64111
(816) 531-3119

For all the blessings this city has given me, and to my mom and dad for encouraging me to follow my heart

CONTENTS

ACKNOWLEDGMENTS

Thanks go to a city of restaurateurs, hotel managers, shop owners, and attraction employees who answered questions, provided information, and helped me fine-tune some of the details of this book.

The well-versed staff in the Nashville Room at the Ben West Public Library also deserve thanks for steering me in the right direction to discover historical facts about Nashville. Barry McAlister at Metro Parks was generous with information and a book about the city's park system. And Tom Adkinson at Opryland was nice enough to provide more than enough details about his environs northeast of the city. Many others also felt obliged to offer a suggestion or reveal information that proved helpful.

My friends and family need to be acknowledged for their interest and advice. In particular, Ed Carter, for brainstorming the title with me, and my sister and brother-in-law, Cindy and Scott Moskovitz, for making it possible for me to move here in the first place.

My husband Lindsay, as well as children Anna and Lily, must be thanked once again for their encouragement and support, and also for bearing with me during the many weekends and evenings I had to excuse myself to my office. Their patience and love made this possible.

INTRODUCTION

People the world over have heard of Nashville. The name is synonymous with country music, and even in the most remote areas of the globe people know of Music City USA.

The city is indeed the capital of country music, and its influence can be seen and felt in the clubs, recording studios, and stores that line the streets. The fast-growing industry helped push Nashville from its rural status to that of a cosmopolitan community, which continues to develop at an accelerated rate.

Nashville is located within 250 miles of 12 states, making it a convenient place to live and visit. Situated in what is referred to as Middle Tennessee, this is the largest metropolitan area in the state, with a population of a little more than a million in the greater Metropolitan Statistical Area (MSA), which includes eight surrounding counties.

Nashville is also the capital of Tennessee, declared so by the legislature in 1843. The capitol building still looms largely over the downtown area and brings scores of politicians, lobbyists, and other government-related officials to the city. And because 1996 is Tennessee's bicentennial, there are all kinds of special events scheduled throughout the state.

This Southern city is often referred to as "the buckle on the Bible Belt" due to the preponderance of churches, religious publishers, and national church offices that operate here. The first record of a church occurred in 1796 on Church Street (of course), and it was an ancestor of the current McKendree Methodist Church. Many are notable for their distinctive architecture, including the Downtown Presbyterian Church, which is the largest and best preserved example of the Egyptian Revival style in this country. And the church leaders of Nashville were responsible for establishing many of the city's educational institutions like Vanderbilt University, Belmont University, and David Lipscomb University. The gospel music industry here also resulted from the strong presence of churches.

In early 1854 Nashville became the first Southern city to establish a public school system. The first institution was Hume School, built where Hume-Fogg High School stands today on Broadway downtown. In the years following, Nashville would become home to Fisk University, Meharry Medical College, and Vanderbilt University. "Athens of the South" is still a moniker used to refer to the well-respected roster of colleges and universities in the area.

The city is also known as a center for the health-care industry because of companies like Columbia/HCA, HealthSouth, and Baptist Health Care Systems. Businesses such as Aladdin Industries, Service Merchandise, Shoney's, and Dollar General are headquartered here, and Nashville is also known for its banking and insurance companies.

And even though country music is Nashville's calling card, a short visit will reveal the city's diversity. Its image, recorded in 1817 by Ann Royall—said to be the first woman journalist in America—still rings true today: "At a distance of a mile from the town you see a board with a hand painted on it as large as life, and the fore finger pointing, with the following inscription in large letters underneath—'Look and see the Town!' Upon looking down the road you see the town sure enough. It has a beautiful appearance when viewed from this point."

VISITOR ASSISTANCE

STAYING COMFORTABLE

Nashville is a casual place, where the dress code ranges from jeans to suits. Only a few of Music City's best restaurants suggest a jacket; otherwise, informal clothing is fine, including shorts in the summer.

Nashville has very distinct seasons, with fairly mild winters and not terrifically hot summers (although some years can be worse than others). July and August can be hot and humid, with average high temperatures around 90 degrees. Sunscreen is always a good idea, and insect repellent can help stave off the mosquitoes during summer evenings. Winter temperatures can fall to single digits, but it's not unusual to experience a 50-degree day occasionally, too. The average low temperatures in January and February are 28 to 30 degrees. Usually less than a half dozen snowfalls occur each year, and the city doesn't fare well when it happens—schools close when flurries appear, and icy roads wreak havoc in all directions. Fall and spring are both exceptionally beautiful times in Music City. The trees burst into color in October, and spring blossoms emerge between mid-March and early April. Most rain comes during the spring months, and often that means flash flood warnings. Allergy sufferers should note that both fall and spring can be brutal seasons. Come prepared.

IF YOU FLY IN

The **Nashville International Airport** is located about eight miles southeast of downtown off Interstate 40 East. The airport Welcome Center can assist you with transportation information and details about Nashville (615-275-1674).

Airlines serving Nashville include Air Canada, AirTran, American, Comair, Continental, Continental Connection, Delta, Northwest, Skyway Airlines, Southwest, TWA, United, USAir, USAir Express, ValueJet, and Western Pacific.

The **Grayline Downtown Airport Express** provides shuttle service to downtown hotels and those on the west side of the city from 6 a.m. to 11 p.m. Fares run about $9 per person one way and $15 round-trip. For information call (615) 275-1180 or (800) 669-9463. A taxi ride from the airport to downtown is about $16 one way for up to five people.

TRANSPORTATION TIPS

First and foremost, Nashvillians (and Tennesseans) are required to use seat belts, so buckle up. In addition, children under four must be restrained in a child safety seat.

The city is organized on a grid system, which continues from downtown for quite a distance even though interrupted by highways and other roads. Three major interstates intersect here—I-40 and I-24 run east and west, I-65 takes drivers north and south—and I-265 and I-440 loop around the city. The area's latest interstate project, I-840, will connect I-40 between many outlying counties.

Nashville's downtown area is fairly easy to maneuver, although some streets are one-way. Numbered *avenues* run parallel to the Cumberland River, and *streets,* which run perpendicular, are named. What makes driving confusing sometimes is the name change that affects many of the busiest thoroughfares. For instance, West End Avenue turns into Harding Road, Broadway changes into 21st Avenue South and then becomes Hillsboro Pike, and Eighth Avenue becomes Franklin Road to the south and MetroCenter Boulevard to the north. A good street map of the city can alleviate any problems you might encounter. And bicyclists should take note: Nashville is not a city with bike paths, so riding can be hazardous.

Conventioneers and others staying at any of the downtown hotels don't need a car for exploring this area. Historic Second Avenue, Lower Broadway, and Printers Alley are all within walking distance of each other. Parking can be difficult, too, so you're almost better off without the hassle of driving or renting a vehicle.

Plus the open-air trolley cars of the **Nashville Trolley Co.** (130 Nestor St., 615-862-5950) can transport you around downtown, Music Row, and even in the Music Valley area, too. The three routes run daily from mid-April through mid-October. During the winter months, trolleys operate on Saturdays for the downtown and Music Row areas. The Music Valley route operates Monday through Saturday during the winter schedule. Trolley singers entertain folks during summer weekends on the Music Row route, and the "Spirits of Nashville" (guides dressed as ghosts who give historical information about the city) are offered during summer weekends on the downtown route. You can get on and off at any stop and pay 90 cents each time.

GUIDED TOURS

Taking a tour of Music City can be a comfortable way to either get an overview of what's here or concentrate on a particular area or interest. Sightseeing or overnight package tours are available from numerous companies located here.

Civil War Tours of Tennessee (6600 Hwy. 100, 615-356-7537) give riders an overview of the importance of the Civil War in Nashville, Franklin, and Spring Hill. Battle sights, historic homes, and other significant locations come to life on the tour.

Country & Western/Gray Line Tours (2416 Music Valley Dr., 615-883-5555 or 800-251-1864) offer star home tours and historical tours as well as occasional holiday excursions.

Grand Ole Opry Tours (2810 Opryland Dr., 615-889-9490) take visitors to famous Nashville sites and attractions, The Hermitage, and country stars' homes.

Johnny Walker Tours (97 Wallace Rd., 615-834-8585 or 800-722-1524) provide city tours and jaunts to country music stars' residences in both Brentwood and Hendersonville.

NASHVILLE CUISINE

Nashville, like much of the South, is steeped in food traditions that start with main dishes like fried chicken, country-fried steak, catfish, and country ham. Add to that a dose of hard-cooked vegetables and casseroles like turnip greens, baked squash, butter beans, or stewed tomatoes, some hot corncakes or biscuits, iced tea, and desserts like chess pie, peach cobbler, sweet potato pie, and coconut cake, and you've sampled the comfort food of the South.

Nashville has a good selection of restaurants called "meat-and-threes," where you can order meat, a couple of vegetables, bread, and a drink. They are inexpensive, filling, and, best of all, made with the same care you'd expect from a meal at someone's home.

Barbecue, a distinctly Southern food, is found at small, modest eateries, where the aroma generally reaches your senses before you can park the car. In Nashville and Tennessee at large, barbecue generally means pork, with cuts like shoulder and ribs. But don't dismiss barbecue chicken, beef brisket, and even turkey, which can be a tasty treat, too.

Even though typical Southern food is well worth eating, there are numerous restaurants in Music City that will satisfy most any hankering. Award-winning Italian, California-influenced salads, wood-fired pizzas, steaks, and all manner of ethnic options dot the city. And many of the more upscale dining spots take our wonderful regional influence and apply it to new, inventive dishes.

ADDITIONAL INFORMATION SOURCES

The **Nashville Convention & Visitors Bureau** (161 Fourth Ave. N., 615-259-4700) is the best source for information about the city. There is a walk-up booth at the Fourth Avenue location, but the main center is situated off Interstate 65, at the foot of the Victory Memorial Bridge on the east side of the Cumberland River (300 Main St., 615-259-4747), and is open daily. The **Nashville Area Chamber of Commerce** (161 Fourth Ave. N., 615-259-4755) is open weekdays and can help with additional information about Music City USA.

The **Nashville Downtown Partnership** (615-259-4763) promotes the downtown area through marketing and managing programs. Look for "downtown ambassadors" from late May through August to guide you through the central business district and help with emergencies.

There is also a **Welcome Center at the Nashville International Airport** (615-275-1674) open daily on the baggage level that can supply you with brochures and other information. A new visitors center will open in the tower of the downtown arena (replacing, when it does, the one in East Nashville) and will offer brochures, merchandise, and public restrooms. Short films about Nashville will be shown in a second floor theater.

The **Bell South Real Yellow Pages** has a "Restaurant and Entertainment Guide" that can be accessed by calling (615) 377-9777. Categories of cuisines as well as specific information on hours and menus for many restaurants are available by phone. Golf, guided tours, nightclubs, theater, and concert updates can also be found by using this service.

Visitors can tap into services for the disabled through the **Disability Information Office** (25 Middleton St., 615-862-6492). Call if you have questions about transportation and accessibility to Nashville businesses and attractions.

Foreign currency exchange is available at several area banks, including First Union Bank (615-251-9200), First American National Bank (615-748-2941), and SunTrust Bank (615-748-4000), and at the Wright Travel Business Center at the Nashville International Airport (615-275-2660).

CULTURAL ARTS/ SPECTATOR SPORTS

CULTURAL ARTS

Classical music, dance, theater, opera, and visual art are all an important part of Music City. Since Nashville has experienced such a growth spurt over the past decade, the cultural arts have been even more fine-tuned, gaining support and interest from the increasing population.

VENUES

Darkhorse Theatre (4610 Charlotte Ave., 615-297-7113) provides a small comfy space in a renovated church for watching much of the community theater that takes place in Nashville. Dance performances are also on tap here.

The **Nashville Arena** (Broadway, between Fifth and Sixth Ave. S., 615-880-2850) will soon open as a destination for sporting events, concerts, family shows, and maybe even a major league sports team.

The **Nashville Municipal Auditorium** (417 Fourth Ave. N., 615-862-6390) hosts a variety of events—ranging from conventions to concerts—and was recently updated with new seats and an ice rink.

Summertime concerts at **Starwood Amphitheatre** (3839 Murfreesboro Pk., 615-641-5800) draw crowds for appearances by big-name performers playing all types of music. James Taylor, Tom Petty, Reba McEntire, and Aaron Neville are some of the musicians that have entertained under the stars. Reserved seating is available, but lots of people like to spread a blanket on the grassy slopes.

The **Tennessee Performing Arts Center** (505 Deaderick St., 615-741-7975), better known as TPAC, is the site for many productions in its three theaters named for Tennessee's U.S. presidents—James K. Polk, Andrew Johnson, and Andrew Jackson. Local theater companies, dance organizations, opera, and musical performances are scheduled throughout the year.

The recently renovated **War Memorial Auditorium** (Seventh Ave. N. and Union St., 615-741-9263) is a small venue with seating for about 1,500. Classical concerts, dance recitals, meetings, and seminars are scheduled at this state-owned facility off Legislative Plaza.

THEATER GROUPS

The following are just some of the theater groups that stage performances during the year.

ACT I (4104 Moss Rose Dr., 615-780-2909), now in its eighth season, offers audiences classic American and European plays five times a year at the Darkhorse Theatre.

American Negro Playwright Theatre (311 Woodwind Ct., 800-923-4925) and founder Barry Scott produce existing and original dramas about the black experience in America.

Circle Players (505 Deaderick St., 615-254-0113) is the city's oldest community theater group (started in 1949) and presents six plays each year, ranging from mysteries to musicals.

Mockingbird Public Theatre (4643 Goodman Rd., Adams, TN 37010, 615-696-9951) entertains audiences with four shows each year, most of which are by Southern theatrical artists.

Nashville Academy Theatre (724 Second Ave. S., 615-254-9103) is the city's venue for children's productions and one of the three oldest continuing professional children's theaters in the country. Since 1931, NAT has produced age-appropriate plays for young audiences from preschool through middle school.

Nashville Ballet (2976 Sidco Dr., 615-244-7233) has for more than 10 years graced the stage with four performances, including the annual holiday treat—*The Nutcracker.*

Shalom Theatre (801 Percy Warner Blvd., 615-356-7170) is based at the Jewish Community Center and produces a varied lineup of plays twice a year. Often the works relate to Judaism in some way or feature Jewish playwrights.

Tennessee Dance Theatre (625-A Seventh Ave. S., 615-248-3262) is known for its season of well-choreographed performances related to Southern themes that travel the state.

Tennessee Repertory Theatre (427 Chestnut St., 615-244-4878) stages five productions annually, ranging from musicals to dramas. Tennessee Rep got its start in 1985 and is the state's largest professional theater.

Theatre Horizons (Church Street Centre, 625 Church St., 615-244-7115) presents 10 to 17 contemporary off-Broadway plays a year, including recent releases and acquisitions.

MUSIC

Blair School of Music (2400 Blakemore Ave., 615-322-7651) offers musical instruction in a variety of instruments and voice as well as concerts throughout the year featuring both students and adults. It is part of Vanderbilt University.

Nashville Opera Association (1900 Belmont Blvd., 615-292-5710), which started in 1981, entertains with three performances each year, including productions like *La Traviata, Die Fledermaus,* and *Tosca.*

Nashville Symphony Orchestra (208 23rd Ave. N., 615-329-3033) is conducted by Kenneth Schermerhorn and offers a well-rounded roster of classical/pop music concerts throughout the year, including summertime concerts in the city's parks and at Cheekwood.

Tennessee Opera Theater (5924 Sedberry Rd., 615-356-7372) has been making opera accessible to audiences since 1988 with two performances each season, always sung in English. TOT focuses on developing up-and-coming regional talent.

SPECTATOR SPORTS

Nashville has been wrestling (pun intended) with trying to get a major league sports team to call the city home for a few years now. The Houston Oilers have agreed to move here, pending completion of a 65,000-seat stadium, set for 1998. The 20,000-seat Nashville Arena will also host a variety of sporting events and may be a draw for a second national sports franchise. In the meantime, there's plenty of action to follow.

AUTO RACING

Nashville Speedway USA (Tennessee State Fairgrounds, 615-726-1818) hosts NASCAR stock car races weekly from April through September on Saturday nights. During October three races are on tap, involving drivers from across the United States and Canada. Call for specific races and dates.

BASEBALL

The **Nashville Sounds** (534 Chestnut St., 615-242-4371) play home games at Greer Stadium, known for its guitar-shaped scoreboard. The Sounds are a Triple A farm team of the Chicago White Sox and play some 72 home games during the season, which runs from early April through early September.

COLLEGE SPORTS

Vanderbilt University competes in the 12-team Southeastern Conference that includes games with Alabama, Florida, and arch-rival University of Tennessee. Dudley Field, located right off West End Avenue, is the site for six home games played from early September through November. The Commodores also draw crowds for both men's and women's basketball, with a season that runs from November through March. Other spectators may want to head to the soccer fields to watch both men's and women's leagues play, or grab a seat to see Vandy's baseball team take to the diamond. For tickets call (615) 322-3544.

Tennessee State University's football team plays in the Ohio Valley Conference, and the Tigers also garner excitement for the men's and women's basketball games (615-963-5861). The Tigerbelles are well known for their record-setting stunts on the track field and for late-great alumna and Olympic star Wilma Rudolph.

David Lipscomb University has one of the hottest basketball teams in the college NAIA circuit (615-269-1822). McQuiddy Gymnasium, located between Granny White Pike and Belmont Boulevard, is the place to see the fast-paced action.

GOLF

There are seven golf courses maintained by **Metro Parks** throughout the city and several other private courses (615-862-8400). Opryland's **Springhouse Golf Club** is the site of the BellSouth Senior Classic and is the stop for Nashville's PGA Tour (18 Springhouse Ln., 615-871-7759). The Sara Lee Classic LPGA Golf Tournament, which features the world's top women golfers, is held each May at the **Hermitage Golf Course** (3939 Old Hickory Blvd., 615-847-4001).

HORSE RACING

The Iroquois Memorial Steeplechase draws throngs of folks to the hillside of **Percy Warner Park** for the annual race, held the second weekend in May (see "Festivals"). The amateur steeplechase benefits Vanderbilt Children's Hospital (615-322-7450).

HOW TO USE THIS GUIDE

Whether you've lived in Nashville all your life, have relocated here recently, or are visiting Music City USA for a short time, this book can help you find your way. It is not meant to cover the entire metropolitan area, but rather to cut through the city to the best in attractions, shopping, dining, nightlife, and accommodations.

There is much about Nashville that makes it unique. From the Grand Ole Opry to Radnor Lake, from meat-and-threes to Fan Fair, this city has a personality and a persona all its own. Nashville has exploded in the last 15 years or so, with exciting changes like a resurrected downtown area, a 20,000-seat arena, and a steady stream of new people who now make Music City their home.

The best way to explore Nashville is gradually and over time. But if you're only here for a week, you can still discover and enjoy some of the sites that make longtime residents proud. Since space limitations prevent going into great detail on every attraction, there are several "Local Treasures" sections sprinkled throughout the book to explain more about places that make Nashville special.

This guide is organized geographically, with subsections on attractions, shopping, dining, nightlife, and accommodations. That way, if you happen to be in Green Hills, the restaurants and stores you might want to visit are all listed under that heading. And if you're spending a day at Opryland USA, you'll be able to find other attractions and nightspots in that section of the city.

And rather than giving specific hours, admission fees, and other details, you'll find the address and phone number provided for each place. It's always best to call ahead to make sure the establishment is still open, the cost hasn't changed, and whether any other particulars may be different. And because Nashville is on the move, there might be some new businesses or attractions that have opened that didn't make it into this edition. You can check with the Nashville Convention & Visitors Bureau, 161 Fourth Avenue N., Nashville, TN 37219, or call (615) 259-4700 for more information.

Because prices are subject to change, the following dollar-sign system will guide you:

Restaurants
$ = Inexpensive ($5 and under)
$$ = Moderate ($5–$15)
$$$ = Expensive (over $15)

Accommodations (for a standard room)
$ = Inexpensive (under $100)
$$ = Moderate ($100–$150)
$$$ = Expensive (over $150)

The symbol ☐ denotes credit card acceptance.

In addition to the various areas of the city, some additional places worth visiting are noted in the "On the Outskirts" chapter. The listings found in "Festivals" can also help you plan weekend outings or investigate new places. Whatever you're looking for, *Nashville Inside Out* should help steer you in the right direction and show you the best of what the city offers.

BELLE MEADE

Belle Meade is unique because of its location right in the middle of Nashville—a separate city, with its own mayor and government. Approximately 3,000 residents live here and are among the movers and shakers of the larger city of Nashville.

Belle Meade Boulevard is the primary thoroughfare in the city, lined on either side by well-manicured lawns and beautiful homes and marked by distinctive black street signs adorned with horses. The Boulevard, which once saw trolley cars moving up and down its length, has become a favorite place for runners and walkers. The Belle Meade Country Club, one of the most exclusive associations in Nashville, is located here, and the picturesque Richland Creek winds through the western edge of the city.

Belle Meade was incorporated in 1938, and no commercial establishments are allowed within the city limits. However, a number of restaurants and businesses operate on Harding Road, on the outskirts of the residential section of the city, which many consider part of the Belle Meade area. City Hall is located at 4705 Harding Road (615-297-6041).

ATTRACTIONS

For a step back in time, you can visit the **Belle Meade Plantation** (5025 Harding Rd., 615-356-0501; admission fee). This Greek Revival mansion completed in 1853 was once world famous for its Thoroughbred nursery and stud farm. Now 30 acres remain of the former 5,400-acre plantation, and several of the buildings have been restored. The mansion itself is outfitted with furnishings from the period, and the carriage house and stable display one of the largest antique carriage collections in the South. The smokehouse, garden house, creamery, and one of the oldest log cabins in Tennessee—dating to 1790—are also open for viewing. The grounds of the Plantation host the annual Fall Fest, featuring arts and crafts, antiques, music, and food (see "Festivals"), and a Victorian Christmas celebration in December. Other lectures and exhibits are also scheduled throughout the year, and the Tennessee Jazz and Blues Society stages concerts here in the summer months.

Another one of Nashville's stately homes is Cheekwood, once the residence of Leslie and Mabel Cheek, members of the Maxwell House coffee family. Now called **Cheekwood: Nashville's Home of**

Art and Gardens (1200 Forrest Park Dr., 615-356-8000; admission fee), the 55 acres showcase woodlands, wildflowers, roses, daylilies, herbs, and even a Japanese-style garden. And the wide expanse of lawns provides a lush backdrop for the "Sounds on the Grounds" summertime musical concerts.

The limestone mansion, which stands at the top of a hill, has been transformed into a museum of art, with a sizable permanent collection of 19th- and 20th-century American paintings, Worcester porcelain, Western art, and American silver in addition to other art and artifacts, including Nashville native William Edmondson's stone sculptures. Although the structure's three floors also serve as a venue for traveling exhibitions, the home is noteworthy in its own right for its distinctive architectural features, including mahogany doors, crystal chandeliers, and a wrought-iron stairway from Queen Charlotte's Palace in Kew, England. Cheekwood's long-range plans call for a sculpture trail and another museum building for temporary exhibitions and its permanent collection. The gardens and educational programs will also be expanded in the coming years. Cheekwood's annual Swan Ball ranks among the city's swankiest events, attracting movers and shakers from around the country.

Botanic Hall is where the horticultural exhibits are held, and the greenhouses contain rare and interesting flora, including camellias, orchids, and cloud forest plants. Crafts, books, and gifts await browsers at the museum shop, and visitors can eat a Southern-style lunch overlooking the gardens in the adjoining Pineapple Room Restaurant (615-352-4859). A variety of special events take place during the year, including the popular Trees of Christmas in December, February's Antiques and Gardens show (see "Festivals"), and the well-attended flower shows in the spring.

One of Belle Meade's nicest play areas is **Parmer Park** (at Leake Ave. and Park Hill; free). Swings, slides, a walking track, a basketball court, and picnic tables under shade trees make this a popular spot for families and mothers' groups. There are plenty of grassy areas for running, and a memorial arch from the original Walter O. Parmer School still stands, offering a great spot for imaginative play.

For biking, walking, hiking, running, horseback riding, or even a quiet drive, take to the hills of **Warner Parks** (entrances on Belle Meade Blvd., Highway 100, Chickering Rd., and Old Hickory Blvd.) Both parks—Percy Warner and Edwin Warner—were named after men who were instrumental in park system development for the city. These parks, which are listed in the National Register of Historic Places, cover some 2,600 acres of land, placing them among the largest municipally operated parks in this country. The Works Progress Administration added many features still visible today, including seven limestone entrances, two stone bridges, picnic shelters, bridle paths, and a steeplechase course, which is the site of the annual Iroquois Steeplechase, one of the country's premiere horse racing events (see "Festivals"). Percy Warner Golf Course and Harpeth Hills Golf Course are located in Percy Warner Park. The Warner Park Nature Center at Edwin Warner offers exhibits and a variety of programs dealing with environmental education, as well as baseball diamonds and a model airplane field, too.

SHOPPING

The American Artisan (4231 Harding Rd., 615-298-4691) is unlike any other store in Nashville. The shop represents artisans from around the country with handmade collectibles in every form. Glassware, dishes, frames, boxes, furniture, a large selection of jewelry, and even children's toys can be found here. The store offers a bridal registry and is responsible for the annual American Artisan Festival in Centennial Park each June (see "Festivals").

The finest handmade linens are available at **Bella Linea** (6031 Hwy. 100, 615-352-4041) in the Westgate Center. Down comforters and pillows, duvets, sheets (with thread counts from 200 to 440), feather beds, hand-painted furniture, mattresses and box springs, custom shutters, draperies, and old-fashioned handmade iron beds are for sale here. Bella Linea will also restore and clean comforters and pillows.

Many Nashvillians were heartbroken when the Belle Meade Theater closed its doors in 1991. But even though there are no more movies to see, shoppers can find their favorite books at **Bookstar** (4301 Harding Rd., 615-292-7895). The marquee remains out front as well as autographed photographs of many of the stars that once passed through the movie house's doors. The steps that led to the theater balcony now take customers to the children's department. Bookstar also has a good selection of magazines and stages book signings on a regular basis.

Coco (4239 Harding Rd., 615-292-0362) is a favorite of some of Nashville's smartest dressers. The shop caters to a broad spectrum of women, with both affordable and high-end apparel. In business some 20 years, Coco also does wardrobe consulting and sells a full line of accessories.

The Corner Market (6051 Hwy. 100, 615-352-6772) is a food lover's haven. A plentiful assortment of gourmet edibles await shoppers as well as some of the best produce around. You'll also find fresh fish, a top-notch selection of cheeses, pâte, and bulk items here in addition to the latest foodstuffs to hit the market. Besides its retail operation, the store hosts cooking classes, wine tastings, and other special events. The Corner Market also features take-out meals (see "Dining") and will design gift baskets.

If you're in the market for fine giftware and jewelry, **Crystal's** (4550 Harding Rd., 615-292-4300) is a good place to explore. The Belle Meade Plaza store gets its name from owner/country singer Crystal Gayle. A tempting selection of Rado watches, top-of-the-line crystal, fine china, frames, stationery, and other gifts can be found here, plus the shop offers both bridal and corporate registries.

Antiques are what draw browsers to **Evelyn Anderson Galleries** (6043 Hwy. 100, 615-352-6770), one of several stores in the Westgate Center that deals in old collectibles. For almost 40 years the business has sold antique porcelains, furniture, rugs, and paintings. There is also a gift area offering good reproductions of antiques.

For designer wear at a discount, check out **The French Shoppe** (6029 Hwy. 100, 615-352-9296). You can find name brands at 30 to 50 percent off as well as accessories like socks, belts, jewelry, and handbags. The store also presents a nice selection of "cotton cashmere" casual clothing.

Jamie (4317 Harding Rd., 615-292-4188) features both American and European designers as well as a contemporary section with labels like DKNY. There's also a shoe salon of high-end footwear, a collection of fine jewelry, a Vera Wang bridal showroom, and a variety of cosmetics.

The women's section of **McClures** (6000 Hwy. 100, 615-356-8822) certainly dominates the store, but this family-owned business also sells great men's and children's clothing, too. McClures has a terrific selection of stylish garments, specializing in designer wear and name brands. The women's shoe department boasts a great selection, too. The store also has unusual gift items, especially during the holiday season.

For knowledgeable service about wine, drive underneath Belle Meade Plaza (near Kroger) and head to **Nashville Wine and Spirits** (4556 Harding Rd., 615-292-2676). Vintages from around the world as well as various liquors are available here, and well-trained employees can help take the guesswork out of pairing food and wine. The store also stages numerous wine tastings (with a variety of restaurants in the city).

You don't have to be a kid to enjoy walking through **Phillips Toy Mart** (5207 Harding Rd., 615-352-5363). Phillips is crammed with a wide selection of playthings, and it hasn't changed much since opening in 1946. Hard-to-find dolls, electric trains, and hobby supplies make the shop worth a stop, especially if you want to escape the Toys R Us crowds.

It's hard to see anything but the Oriental rugs and tapestries in **Ro's Oriental Rugs** (6602 Hwy. 100, 615-352-9055). The small shop, owned by Rosalie Buxbaum, is the place to find the finest rugs and tapestries for your home or office. Ro's is one of several antique stores located on a strip of Highway 100.

Art lovers will discover an excellent selection at **Shelton Gallery & Frame** (4239 Harding Rd., 615-298-9935) in the Stanford Square shopping area. Shelton carries American folk art, West African tribal art, Haitian art, and the lithographs and original drawings of internationally known New York artist Red Grooms (a former Nashvillian). The gallery conducts openings and rotating exhibitions.

You can find all your outdoor needs at **Sports and Trails** (108 Page Rd., 615-356-2300). Hiking boots, outerwear, books, tents, backpacks, rock climbing gear, and other equipment is sold here, and the store conducts trips and offers workshops throughout the year.

When a flower arrangement takes your breath away, it's usually the work of **The Tulip Tree** (6025 Hwy. 100, 615-352-1466). One of Nashville's better florists for more than 25 years, The Tulip Tree uses unusual European flowers, which are direct shipped from Holland, in its designs. Fresh-cut flowers, bedding plants, and a variety of gifts are also sold at this Westgate Center store, and the establishment decorates for weddings and parties as well.

What's old is new again at **Zelda** (5133 Harding Rd., 615-356-2430), where you can find vintage pieces from the '20s, '30s, and '40s as well as the shop's own designs. The Belle Meade Galleria store also stages periodic trunk shows.

DINING

Diners can enjoy the culinary expertise of one of Nashville's best-known chefs, Robert Siegel, at the **Belle Meade Brasserie** (101 Page Rd., 615-356-5450; $$–$$$, □). This cozy bistro gives customers a taste of Siegel's inventive combinations with dishes like crab-stuffed shrimp or sage and apple grilled veal chop. There's a pleasant outdoor patio for dining that attracts folks from the neighborhood, and the Brasserie also has an award-winning wine list.

Belle Meade Buffet Cafeteria (4534 Harding Rd., 615-298-5571; $$), established in 1961, is a place where the choices can make you experience vertigo. The food line begins with meringue-topped pies (but don't let that fool you—there are more sweets at the end), and then come the salads, meats, vegetables, rolls, and drinks. You can make a meal here just on vegetables, with selections that range from squash casserole to whipped yams. Whatever you pick, a waiter carries your tray to a table in the large dining room (a tip is customary) where you can then dig in.

Fresh-baked bread like that enjoyed in the European countryside is what **Bread & Company** (106 Page Rd., 615-352-7323; $, □) does best. Cinnamon-raisin, rosemary-olive, sesame semolina, and whole wheat farm are just a sampling of what this bakery churns out daily. In addition, there's a tempting assortment of rolls, muffins, and incredible pastries as well as interesting sandwiches like marinated mozzarella and herb-roasted turkey breast (served on Bread & Company bread, of course).

Belle Meade finally got a place to buy bagels, cream cheese, and deli sandwiches when **Bruegger's Bagel Bakery** opened (5305 Harding Rd., 615-352-1128; $). Bruegger's 13 varieties are baked all day long in an open-hearth oven. There are also specialty coffees, salads, soups, and desserts on the eatery's menu.

Lunch is a treat at **The Corner Market** (6051 Hwy. 100, 615-352-6772; $, □), where you can find specialty sandwiches like a muffuletta, a BLT, or a "veggywich" of avocado, Swiss cheese, tomato, sprouts, and lettuce. You'll have a hard time passing up the Eclectic Tossed Salad, which combines greens, berries, almonds, blue cheese, scallions, and avocado in a sesame vinaigrette, or the chef's delicious seafood gumbo (always available on Saturdays). The homemade soups and desserts are also worth sampling. The Corner Market does catering and consulting, too, and has already-prepared entrees to take home to your own dinner table.

Finezza Trattoria (5405 Harding Rd., 615-356-9398; $$, □) is a casual Italian dining spot that serves up tasty fare at reasonable prices. Try the chicken-tortellini soup, Ziti Rustica, or some of the other Italian country dishes, but first nibble some of the fresh-baked bread dipped in garlic-infused olive oil while you wait. Don't leave without a piece of authentic *tiramisu,* the traditional Italian dessert. There's even a kid's menu, too.

Tucked back in the Belle Meade Plaza is **Goldie's Deli** (4520 Harding Rd., 615-292-3589; $$, □), located where Schwartz's Delicatessen used to be. Traditional deli fare like matzo ball soup, New York–style sandwiches, stuffed cabbage, and salami and eggs greets diners. Goldie's also stocks kosher food staples, has a full deli counter, and offers catering.

Back in the right-hand corner of Belle Meade Drugs is **The Picnic Cafe** (4334 Harding Rd., 615-297-5398; $), where you can munch on salads, deli sandwiches, and tasty banana-nut muffins or homemade cheese wafers. Lemon squares, chess tarts, or Kathy's crescents will round out your meal. The Picnic is a cheery spot, with blue-and-white-checked tablecloths and great tea punch. The eatery makes up lunch boxes to go if you're in a hurry, and it also offers catering.

You don't have to be a sports enthusiast to want to visit **Sportsman's Grille** (5405 Harding Rd., 615-356-6206; $$, ☐). The burgers with grilled onions are top-notch, and the Grille also offers catfish, ribs, steak, and a good assortment of salads. Although televisions tune you in to whatever sporting event is in play, the noise level may allow you to just watch, not listen.

Belle Meade residents (and the rest of the city) like **Sperry's** (5109 Harding Rd., 615-353-0809; $$, ☐) for its dark, cozy interior and familiar fare. Here you're almost certain to see someone you know if you live in the area. Steaks, seafood, prime rib, and a fresh salad bar (one of the few with Green Goddess dressing) make up the menu, and there's a homey bar on one side where locals have gathered since 1974.

BELLEVUE

Bellevue, which lies southwest of Nashville, celebrated its 200th year of settlement in 1995. The fast-growing area still seems quite rural, even as the next millennium approaches. But more and more stores and restaurants are opening in this 'burb, and many families opt for its affordable housing and convenience. Bellevue has its own Chamber of Commerce at 156-A Belle Forest Circle (615-662-2737).

ATTRACTIONS

The **Bellevue Greenway** (Old Harding Pk. and Morton Mill Rd.; free) is a scenic place to stroll or run, part of the ongoing efforts of the Metro Greenways Commission to establish these grassy areas in the city. The Bellevue Greenway runs along the Harpeth River and offers 800 feet of boardwalk, a cliff-hugging overlook, and both paved and mulched trails.

The striking architecture of the **Ganesha Temple** (521 Old Hickory Blvd., 615-356-7207; free) causes drivers on Old Hickory Boulevard to slow down. This Hindu temple, which was based on sixth-century design and built in 1992, serves approximately 500 families in the Metro Nashville area. Tours are conducted on Thursday afternoons and Saturdays with advance notice and include a lecture about Hindu philosophy and religion.

There's no end to what motivated citizens can do when they put their time and talent behind something they think is needed. That was how **Red Caboose Park** (Hwy. 70 S. and Colice Jeanne Rd.) came about, when a group of volunteers built the play area in five days. It contains wooden castles, swinging bridges, trains, and a whole host of other creative equipment for kids. The playground complies with the Americans with Disabilities Act.

SHOPPING

The **Bellevue Center** (7620 Hwy. 70 S., 615-646-8690) was the talk of the town when it opened in 1990. The attractive mall of 150 stores still draws folks from the area, especially due to its easy access from Interstate 40. A few of the center's tenants have their only location here, including places like Caswell-Massey, Brentano's Bookstore, the Tennessee Museum Store, and Everything But Water. Roo's Playland, in the center court, is a fun area for kids, with a soft sculpture (and socks-only) gameboard built for climbing, sliding, and jumping.

The Produce Place (7107 Hwy. 70 S., 615-662-1184) offers a terrific source for the ripest tomatoes, Silver Queen corn, apples, berries, and other farm-fresh produce. This pleasant grocery also stocks a wide array of health foods, cheeses, coffees, spices, teas, and other items you might not find at your nearby supermarket. Another location operates at 4000 Murphy Road, off of West End Avenue.

DINING

Fine Italian cuisine is in store for diners at **Antonio's of Nashville** (7097 Old Harding Rd., 646-9166; $$–$$$, □). Most of Antonio's menu reflects the fare of Northern Italy, although some Southern regional dishes are offered, too. Veal, fresh seafood, well-crafted pasta combinations, and steak are on tap, as well as an award-winning shrimp bisque soup. There is outdoor seating, and desserts are all made in-house.

From the family who started Uncle Bud's Catfish restaurant (then sold it 10 years later) comes **Catfish Express** (7609 Hwy. 70 S., 662-1007; $–$$), a tiny take-out place selling grain-fed, farm-raised catfish fillets, hush puppies, coleslaw, and Nick's Famous Barbecue. If you want to put a meal on the table and don't have time to cook, this is a convenient place to grab dinner.

Another Bellevue eatery fills you up with pulled pork, chicken, and even country ham, but not without a full complement of side orders such as Southern-style vegetables, cheesy potatoes, corncakes, and cooked apples. At **Country Cabin Bar-B-Que** (7093 Old Harding Pk., 615-662-1553; $–$$, □), you can motor through the drive-through window or dine inside. A children's menu makes a visit even more tempting for all ages.

The **Loveless Motel and Restaurant** (8400 Hwy. 100, 615-646-9700; $–$$) is nothing less than a Nashville institution. Generations of families (and a host of country music stars) have made the journey to the country for some of this eatery's famous country ham, fried chicken, biscuits, and homemade peach and blackberry preserves ever since it opened in 1951. The small dining spot (the motel is closed) packs them in for breakfast, lunch, and dinner, so reservations are recommended and necessary on weekends. You can buy some of the terrific jam while you're there or take home a mail-order catalog. Gift boxes are available, and the restaurant caters, too.

Nashville's bagel business has boomed in the past couple of years, and one of the places serving Bellevue is **Bagel Gallery** (7079 Hwy. 70

S., 646-1972; $). More than a dozen varieties are baked fresh here, plus there are great blended cream cheeses to buy, too. In addition, try their deli sandwiches. Planning a get-together? The eatery can also make up platters to feed a crowd.

NIGHTLIFE

For almost 30 years **Chaffin's Barn Dinner Theatre** (8204 Hwy. 100, 615-646-9977) has been entertaining audiences with professional productions, including both familiar Broadway plays and comedies, but the place also draws folks to the country for the all-you-can-eat, Southern-style buffet. Chaffin's presents about 10 productions a year on the main stage and another five in the back theater. There are seasonal memberships and occasional matinees as well.

BELMONT

The Belmont area is home to one of Nashville's many institutions of higher learning—Belmont University—which is affiliated with the Southern Baptist Convention. In recent years the school has expanded in acreage and students, the latter now numbering about 3,000. The university is known for its music business program and the Jack Massey Graduate School of Business, named for one of Nashville's most successful entrepreneurs. The most historical building at the university is the Belmont Mansion, the former home of Colonel Joseph and Adelicia Acklen.

This region was once known as a "streetcar suburb" because of the railway line that ran up Belmont Boulevard. The thoroughfare now has a small concentration of shops and restaurants, but most of its length showcases an interesting mix of homes, including bungalows, four-squares, craftsman cottages, and English Tudor Revival structures. At the opposite end of the street, you'll find the campus of David Lipscomb University, located between Belmont Boulevard and Granny White Pike. The school has approximately 2,500 students and is a commuter-based institution.

ATTRACTIONS

The **Belmont Mansion** (1900 Belmont Blvd., 615-386-4459; admission fee) was the ornate Italianate villa constructed in 1850 as Colonel Joseph and Adelicia Acklen's summer home. Reputed to be the wealthiest woman in the United States in the mid-19th century, the residence showcased Adelicia's lavish taste. She owned six plantations in Louisiana, 50,000 acres in Texas, and land in Tennessee. The mansion featured Corinthian columns, fine paintings, marble fountains, cast-iron gazebos, formal gardens, an art gallery, a deer park, a zoo, a bear house, and a bowling alley for entertaining guests. The only structure that still stands (besides the mansion) is the 105-foot water tower used by Federal soldiers to relay signals during the Civil War. Belmont Mansion, listed in the National Register of Historic Places, was sold in 1887 and became the central building for Belmont Junior College for Girls, which later was named Ward-Belmont, Belmont College, and now Belmont University.

SHOPPING

Whatever your sport, the **Athlete's House** (1700 Portland Ave., 615-298-4495) can help find the equipment you need. The store offers a huge selection of athletic footwear and even handles large sizes, plus a wide range of clothing. Personal service has also helped set this shop apart for more than 20 years.

You just have to look in the window of **Helios Artglassworks** (3108 Belmont Blvd., 615-297-5676) to see the handiwork of the stained-glass artists who work here. The store creates custom beveled, etched, and stained glass with both traditional and innovative designs. An in-house gallery features various local artists, and a stop usually allows you to see the craftspeople at work.

The **Green Hills Meat Market** (4004 Granny White Pk., 615-383-7242) isn't really in Green Hills, but it used to be. Now the butcher/gourmet food shop makes its home in a strip of stores that time forgot, across from David Lipscomb University. The meat market carries great-tasting marinated chicken, sun-dried tomato and basil Italian sausage, and a small selection of foodstuffs, including pastas, vinegars, jellies, and fresh produce. The shop also makes deli sandwiches.

The small group of shops where the market operates is a throwback to the 1950s, when personal service meant more than it does today. Shoppers will find a beauty salon, a dry cleaner, a hardware store, a jeweler, and a barber shop here. If you're in the area, stop in at **Hutcherson's Pharmacy** (615-292-4489) for a milkshake made the old-fashioned way.

If you're in the market for imported items from South America, don't miss **Pangaea** (3203 Belmont Blvd., 615-269-9665). Terrific dresses, scarves, belts, and jewelry await shoppers, as do some unusual gifts. There's also a collection of used clothing at the store, and the owner's big (but friendly) dog is often there to greet customers.

Right next door is **Sunshine Grocery** (3201 Belmont Blvd., 615-297-5100), hard to miss due to its purple-painted exterior. This is Nashville's best health-food store, where you can discover organic produce, foods in bulk, natural beauty aids, frozen foods, and other staples. Fresh-baked breads, natural cheeses, baby food, cookbooks, and greeting cards are also available. People line up with containers for Sunshine's water (which is city water that goes through an involved cleaning process), and the grocery's deli yields some terrific edibles, too (see "Dining").

DINING

Bongo Java (2007 Belmont Blvd., 615-385-5282; $) is the place to tank up on espresso and other flavored coffees or to sip a cup of Island Passion tea. The converted house has outdoor tables on the front porch and picnic tables in the yard as well as two levels inside for enjoying some java. This hip spot plays host to a variety of events, including poetry readings, art exhibits, and themed dinners. If you're hungry, the coffeehouse serves sandwiches, salads, homemade soups, and delicious desserts. Or stop by on Sunday for brunch and be surprised with entrees like apricot-mango-stuffed French toast or vegetarian lasagna.

For more than 20 years, **International Market & Restaurant** (2010 Belmont Blvd., 615-297-4453; $–$$, ☐) has been feeding the city a taste of the Far East. The steam tables are full of appetizing Americanized Thai food, and you can order more traditional fare from the kitchen, like *pad Thai* and garlic chicken, best washed down with International Market's papaya juice. Asian grocery products and gifts available are for purchase, too. Across the street is International House, where Thai cooking classes and catered parties are held.

Some say they resemble those found in the Big Apple, but even if not, the pizzas at **Pizza Perfect** (4002 Granny White Pk., 615-297-0345; $–$$, ☐) are worth sampling. You can also bite into an Italian sub or burger here, as well as spaghetti, calzones, and manicotti. Pizza Perfect, which opened in the early '80s, is across the street from David Lipscomb University.

Sunshine Grocery (3201 Belmont Blvd., 615-297-5100; $, ☐) is Nashville's only vegetarian deli, with great daily specials, ready-made sandwiches (try the cheddar/avocado), salads, desserts, and a juice bar. Take home some black bean salad or a broccoli-cheese calzone for a healthy lunch or dinner.

Hungry for tortellini or falafel? Then check out **Tabouli's** (2015 Belmont Blvd., 615-386-0106; $–$$, ☐). This neighborhood eatery serves up inexpensive Mediterranean food, with a good selection of both Italian and Middle Eastern entrees, sandwiches, pizza, and desserts.

BRENTWOOD/
COOL SPRINGS

This rapidly growing area south of Nashville has developed into a bustling community, with much of Brentwood and surrounding Williamson County earning among the highest per capita incomes in the state. Here you'll see a mix of old and new, with stately antebellum homes as neighbors to the many new subdivisions cropping up. The Maryland Farms office complex houses a large number of companies, and the city's public library is located at one end of the thoroughfare that cuts through the buildings. You can take a driving tour to see some of the older structures, most of which are private homes and not open to the public but with historical markers out front explaining their significance. Call the Brentwood Chamber of Commerce, 5211 Maryland Way, at (615) 373-1595, or the Williamson County Tourism Office, City Hall, Franklin, at (615) 794-1225, for a brochure. Several of the tour bus operators take visitors by the Brentwood homes of Alan Jackson, Faith Hill, Dolly Parton, Kix Brooks, and Ronnie Dunn if you want a glimpse of how that half lives (see "Guided Tours" in the Introduction).

ATTRACTIONS

The **Brentwood Community Playground** at **Crockett Park** (Crockett Rd., 615-371-2208; free) draws families to climb on the intricate assemblage of wooden arches, stairs, castles, and other equipment that keeps kids busy and active. There are also baseball fields, soccer/football fields, walking trails, picnic tables, and mulched nature trails dotting the 150-acre park.

The **Brentwood Skate Center** (402 Wilson Pike Cr., 615-373-1827/615-373-8611; admission fee) attracts kids from all over the city for roller skating. The Skate Center offers a variety of skating schedules for families, teen-agers, and even little ones. It's a popular spot for birthday parties, and there are concessions, arcade games, and skate rentals available.

The **Classic Rock Gym** (121 Seaboard Ln., 615-661-9444; admission fee) is the area's largest indoor rock-climbing facility, with more than 5,000 square feet of climbing walls. All levels of experience can enjoy the thrill of scaling a rock face, and there's even an advanced bouldering pit. An in-house pro shop, equipment rental, and instruction are all available.

On a hilltop off of Granny White Pike, stargazers will want to check out Vanderbilt University's **Arthur J. Dyer Observatory** (1000 Oman Dr., 615-373-4897; free). Once a month from March through November, the public can come take a look at celestial bodies through the observatory's two large telescopes. On-site programs, which include video presentations and lectures by university professors, range from meteorites to galaxies and creation. The Dyer Observatory, which was built in 1953, boasts one of the best astronomical libraries in the country, and it's a valuable resource for academic research and study. Two evenings in the fall and spring, classes of students in grades five through eight are invited to visit, with prior arrangements made by teachers.

You can amuse the kids for hours at **Recreation World** (7115 S. Springs Dr., 615-771-7780). Bumper cars, go-carts, miniature golf, and batting cages are offered in addition to a large game room and food court. There's also a state-of-the-art in-line skating facility called the "Rollerdome" here, where in-line skating leagues have tournaments and novice skaters can practice blading.

SHOPPING

At the **CoolSprings Galleria** (1800 Galleria Blvd., 615-771-2050 or 771-2128), shoppers can find more than 100 stores, ranging from Castner Knott to Eddie Bauer and Ann Taylor. Parisan's has its only location here. Every Saturday morning there is a children's story hour, and the mall has periodic fashion shows and other events. In addition to the multitude of retailers here, several strip centers adjacent to the Galleria house discount stores, small shops, and a 10-screen theater. This area is growing dramatically, with many new retail stores planned for the future. The complex is easily accessible off I-65 South.

At **Inside-Out Home Furnishings** (149 Wilson Pk., 615-373-8313) you can decorate both the interior and exterior of your house. There's a substantial selection of patio furniture, as well as upholstery fabrics and household collectibles.

You can find designer clothing for the whole family at **McClures** (257 Franklin Rd., 615-377-3769), a locally owned department store. You can count on McClures for the latest styles, along with a terrific assortment of accessories and shoes. Stop next door at The Outlet for end-of-the-season items, markdowns, and fashions at a discount.

DINING

Barcelona (330 Franklin Rd., 615-377-6527; $$–$$$, ☐) is the city's only Spanish restaurant, with a varied menu of tapas, salads, house specialties, and *paellas*. Everything from steamed mussels to Basque-style haddock is offered, including a couple different flavors of flan, the traditional custard-based dessert. A well-decorated interior makes it easy to forget you're in a strip shopping center.

In the same center you will find **Bruegger's Bagel Bakery** (330 Franklin Rd., 615-661-5668; $), one of the nation's leading bagel chains based in Burlington, Vermont. Stop by for bagels, which are baked all day long in an open-hearth oven, cream cheese, deli sandwiches, soups, salads, desserts, and specialty coffees.

And if you're in the mood for home cooking, **City Cafe** (330 Franklin Rd., 615-373-5555; $–$$) also makes its home in the Brentwood Place shopping center. Plate lunches here combine dishes like roast beef, pork chops, salmon croquettes, and baked ham with a slew of Southern-style side dishes, including stewed raisins and deviled eggs. Round out your meal with the eatery's homemade rolls, cobbler, or pie.

For Memphis-style barbecue, try **Corky's Bar-B-Q** (100 Franklin Rd., 615-373-1020; $$, ☐). Both wet and dry ribs are on tap, in addition to pork shoulder, shrimp, hot tamales, chicken, spaghetti, and a brisket plate. Side orders include barbecue beans, coleslaw, onion loaves, and french fries. Corky's has a drive-through window, can accommodate bulk orders, and offers catering.

It's hard to go wrong when you combine a festive atmosphere with authentic Mexican food, and that's just what **Cozymel's** (1654 Westgate Cr., 615-377-6363; $$, ☐) does. Specializing in dishes from the Yucatán peninsula, the restaurant also serves up 12 different flavors of frozen margaritas. The Dallas-based chain sports a gift shop brimming with Mexican-made items and serves both lunch and dinner.

Sports-bar fans like to visit **Cross Corner Bar & Grill** (127 Franklin Rd., 615-370-0870; $–$$, ☐). Hot wings, nachos, chili, burgers, sandwiches, and a bevy of brews make this a lively place to grab lunch or dinner.

There's a quiet air and calmness about the **East India Club** (4926 Thoroughbred Ln., 615-661-9919; $$, ☐) that makes it a pleasant place to dine. Head in for the lunch buffet and sample traditional Indian fare—*dal, nan,* rice, tandoori chicken, and curries. A full menu awaits diners in the evening with selections like *Chicken Shahi Korma* and *Mattar Paneer.*

Bagels and deli sandwiches draw folks to **Phillip's Delicatessen** (5015 Harpeth Dr., 615-371-9895; $, □). Soups and salads complement creations like the Turkey Reuben, Pastrami Deluxe, and Muffuletta Supreme. Phillip's sells salads by the pound, and bagels in flavors ranging from onion–poppy seed to cherry.

The Puffy Muffin (231 Franklin Rd., 615-373-2741; $–$$, □) is a modern-style tea room that satisfies diners at breakfast and lunch with choices like tortilla soup, Caribbean chicken and black bean salad, crunchy chicken casserole, and Cajun roll-ups. A simple grilled cheese or tuna sandwich is offered, too. Be sure to take home some of the Puffy Muffin's delicious baked goods, or stop in for a slice of pie and a cappuccino.

The jovial atmosphere of **Romano's Macaroni Grill** (1712 Galleria Blvd., 615-771-7002; $–$$, □) makes this Cool Springs restaurant a fun dining spot for the whole family. On top of that, the Italian fare is tasty, varying from pasta and pizza to fish, veal, and chicken dishes. Many of the entrees are based on family recipes, too, and change with the season. A jug of wine in the middle of table is available on the honor system, and waiters may even be motivated to come by and sing an aria. The glass cases of sausages, pasta, and fish on view as you enter make for interesting conversation while you wait for a table.

ACCOMMODATIONS

There are a number of hotels in Brentwood that provide easy access to Nashville and Franklin, Tennessee.

Courtyard by Marriott (103 E. Park Dr., 615-371-9200; $, □) is a comfortable place to stay, with 145 rooms, an outdoor pool, a lounge, and a restaurant that serves breakfast and lunch. It's within walking distance to the many stores and restaurants in the Merchant's Walk shopping center across the street.

The **English Manor Bed and Breakfast** (6304 Murray Ln., 615-373-4627 or 800-332-4640; $–$$, □) is a Southern-style home in a country setting. There are seven rooms with private baths that come with a hearty breakfast, turndown service, and afternoon tea. English Manor has facilities for banquets and meetings, and also offers honeymoon packages.

If you like having a little more space to move around, book your lodgings at **Hilton Suites** (9000 Overlook Blvd. 615-370-0111; $–$$,

□). Here the 200 two-room suites include a refrigerator, microwave oven, and coffee maker as well as a free full breakfast and cocktails in the evening. There's also a fitness center, an indoor pool, a restaurant, and a lounge. Ask about special weekend packages.

The **Brentwood Holiday Inn** (760 Old Hickory Blvd., 615-373-2600; $$–$$$; □) has nearly 250 rooms on its eight floors, a restaurant and lounge, an outdoor pool, a spa and exercise room, and a rental car agency on the premises.

THE DISTRICT

"The District," the catch-all phrase coined in 1990 for the downtown area of Second Avenue (known as Market Street until 1903), Broadway, and Printers Alley, has seen rapid growth in the past couple of years. Second Avenue North in particular seems to be riding the wave of new businesses, making the historic street barely recognizable to longtime residents. Many of the Victorian warehouses, built between 1870 and 1890, have been renovated and now house offices, restaurants, and retail shops. Most of the buildings stretch to First Avenue North, and some can be accessed from that side as well. Wider sidewalks and two-way streets are recent changes made to better accommodate tourists.

Lower Broadway, which was the city's furniture and hardware center in the early days, also boasts some of Nashville's finest Victorian commercial architecture. Restaurants, shops, honky-tonks, and even pawnshops line the street, which once had even more tourist and Opry-related businesses when the Grand Ole Opry used to broadcast from the nearby Ryman Auditorium.

Printers Alley, located between Third Avenue North and Fourth Avenue North, gets its name because of all of the printing and publishing businesses that thrived there in the early 1900s. Way back when, the alley was a hitching post for men bound for the courthouse. In the Victorian years, part of Printers Alley was called the Men's Quarter because of all of the saloons and gambling parlors there. Recently the stretch has experienced a rebirth of sorts, with upgrades like new signage and lighting courtesy of the Metro Council. Now the narrow cobblestone thoroughfare is a hotbed of music and entertainment, just as it was when nightclubs opened there in the 1940s.

Once completed, the 20,000-seat Nashville Arena will bring in concerts, family shows, sporting events, conventions, and maybe even major league sports to the site on Lower Broad. The arena will be open for tours, and there will be a food court and the Tennessee Sports Hall of Fame located inside. The structure promises to alter the downtown landscape even further by bringing more people (and cars) to the busy District. (The Nashville Convention & Visitors Bureau will have an information booth on the first floor of the tower once the arena opens.)

The **Metropolitan Historical Commission** (209 10th Ave. S., 615-862-7970) can provide brochures and other information about The

District. There are three self-guided walking tours on the art and architecture of downtown (pick up a pamphlet before heading out). The City Walk, which leads visitors past places like the Tennessee State Museum, Hatch Show Print, and the Historic Black Business District, is a two-mile walk that traces Nashville's history. Start at Fort Nashborough and follow the painted green line through downtown to 15 different sites, most of which are free and open to the public.

The **Nashville Trolley Co./Metropolitan Transit Authority** (615-862-5950) makes it easy to navigate through downtown. The open-air trolleys, which are more like small buses, provide a pleasant way to see the city or catch a ride to a point of interest (see "Transportation Tips" in the Introduction).

You can also take a 20- to 25-minute guided tour of downtown via horse and carriage. The picturesque white and black conveyances, which are run by **Nashville Carriage Service** (615-670-6330 or 390-5490 evenings), start at Riverfront Park and then head up Broadway to Fifth Avenue. The tour then takes riders up to Commerce Street, down to Second Avenue, onto Church Street, and then down First Avenue to Riverfront Park. Reservations are usually recommended on weekends.

ATTRACTIONS

The **Belle Carol Riverboats** (106 First Ave. S., 615-244-3430 or 800-342-2355; admission fee), docked right downtown, head along the Cumberland River for sightseeing, dinner, and Sunday brunch cruises from March through December. The *Music City Queen* and *Captain Ann* paddle wheelers offer passengers food, entertainment, and history lessons about the city.

Fort Nashborough (170 First Ave. N., 615-862-8400; free) marks the site where Nashville began in 1780. This replica of the fort, built in the 1930s, gives people a look at pioneer life by viewing some of the personal items used during that period in the self-guided tour of the reconstructed settlement.

At **Laser Quest** (166 Second Ave. N., 615-256-2560; admission fee) you can play interactive laser tag in a three-level maze. When you tire of that, head to the arcade for video games, pool tables, and more.

Riverfront Park (Broadway and First Ave. N.) is a one-and-a-half acre tract at the foot of Broadway, easily spotted by the waving flags around a circular drive. The park was conceived as a reminder of the city's 200th birthday and its river heritage. There is a walkway down by the Cumberland River where most of the city's cruise boats dock. The place is popular in the warmer months for the "Dancin' in the District" series of concerts and other musical events (see "Festivals"). It's also where you can catch the Opryland USA River Taxis for a trip to the massive entertainment/hotel complex.

The Riverfront area will attract even more people when the **Tennessee Fox Trot Carousel** (Riverfront Park; admission fee) is put into place. The carousel, a creation of former Nashville resident and now New York artist Red Grooms, will offer visitors a ride on some of the state and city's most beloved athletes, artists, heroes, and legends. Minnie Pearl, Roy Acuff, Davy Crockett, Kitty Wells, Lula Naff, and possibly even a chigger will be represented on the $1.75 million project.

SHOPPING

Furniture shoppers will want to take a look through **A Sofa Shop** (217 Broadway, 615-242-6008) for great contemporary furnishings, including all types of accessories. For antique and upholstered pieces, check out **Circa** (120 Third Ave. S., 615-259-0140), located right off Broadway and owned by the same proprietors.

A Thousand Faces (115 Second Ave. N., 615-259-3919) provides an interesting medley of contemporary gifts, including candles, cards, T-shirts, silver jewelry, scented oils, mirrors, and small pieces of furniture. Check out the store's other location in Hillsboro Village.

Butler's Run (138 Second Ave. N., 615-742-3656) offers a fun array of shops, including **Cinemonde** (615-742-3048), which carries country-and-western memorabilia, movie posters, celebrity photos, and autographs; **Musee de Maillie** (615-256-6794), a gallery showing works by well-known local artist and owner Myles Maillie and other regional artists; and **Southwest & Beyond** (615-259-2878), a store with hand-crafted Native American items, ethnic fashions, and a large selection of products with chili pepper insignia.

The downtown location of **Dangerous Threads** (105 Second Ave. N., 615-256-1033) has the same cutting-edge clothing as their store on West End Avenue. Dare to be different with leather, custom-made garments, and accessories that will make people take notice.

The Great Escape/The Marty Party Headquarters (112 Second Ave. N. in the Market Street Emporium, 615-255-5313) buys and sells CDs, tapes, records, videos, baseball cards, and comic books. In addition, this location serves as a souvenir shop for country artist Marty Stuart. Fans can even see an itinerary of Stuart's upcoming shows.

Gruhn Guitars (400 Broadway, 615-256-2033) is well known worldwide for selling vintage instruments, including both acoustic and electric guitars, banjos, and mandolins. You can also find reissues of favorite musicians' instruments at this collector's haven.

Hatch Show Print (316 Broadway, 615-256-2805) is one of America's oldest surviving show poster printers. It was started in 1879 by two brothers who printed posters for everything from vaudeville shows to traveling evangelists to sporting events. Hatch became the official Grand Ole Opry printer in 1938. Now owned and operated by the Country Music Foundation, Hatch Show Print is a museum and print shop where visitors can see antique printing presses as well as exhibits on the business's history.

Market Street Mercantile (111 Second Ave. S., 615-251-4092) draws tourists in for the cowboy hats, cookbooks, Western jewelry, tipsy cakes, and Nashville souvenirs. Or is it the hay-covered floor?

At **Whoa's on 2nd/The Garth Store** (180 Second Ave. N., 615-726-0037 or 244-1203), shoppers can browse the custom Western apparel, silver jewelry, country music merchandise, and Western sculpture. The lower level stocks Garth Brooks tour merchandise and souvenirs.

DINING

One of the newest dining spots/nightclubs to enter Music City is **B.B. King's Blues Club & Restaurant** (105 Broadway; $$, □). "The Best Place for a Taste of the Blues" serves up red beans and rice, gumbo, fried dill pickles, catfish, barbecue ribs, a Lucille Burger, and other Southern specialties. Blues master B.B. King will appear here at least three or four times a year, and other blues artists will entertain diners as well.

The **Big River Grille & Brewing Works** (111 Broadway, 615-251-4677; $$, □) is one of Nashville's better brew pubs. Try some of the hand-crafted beer (they also make homemade cream soda, root beer, and ginger ale) while munching on entrees like jerk chicken, smoked chicken quesadillas, or the beer barrel shrimp. The house-made sausages are definitely worth sampling, as is the mud pie.

You can ride the rails and enjoy a four-course dinner on the **Broadway Dinner Train** (Riverfront Park, 615-254-8000; $$$, □). Choose between five different entrees like smoked prime rib, grilled salmon, or a special vegetarian dish prepared on the two-and-a-half hour ride to Old Hickory, Tennessee, and back. Tables seat four (or pay extra for a two-top), and reservations are required with payment in advance. Live entertainment is also on tap on the restored 1940s train, which is available for private parties.

The Captain's Table (209 Printers Alley, 251-9535; $$–$$$, ☐) has been dishing out food and music since it opened in Printers Alley in 1946. The romantic banquettes, overstuffed chairs, linen tablecloths, pewter water goblets, and entrees like prime rib, lobster, and rainbow trout remind diners of the old supper clubs. There is a lunch buffet on Fridays, and entertainment in the evening.

When the **Hard Rock Cafe** (100 Broadway, 615-742-9900; $$, ☐) opened downtown in 1994, it signaled a new era for Nashville according to some. Rock memorabilia paired with American cuisine is what makes these restaurants popular the world over. Nashville's Hard Rock is hard to miss because of the large painted mural that looms over the restaurant. A gift shop with Hard Rock memorabilia is located next door in the old Silver Dollar Saloon, which has kept its original tile floor thanks to restoration by the Hard Rock.

Henry's (318-A Broadway, 615-742-6343; $–$$, ☐), one of Lower Broad's newest tenants, touts itself as a traditional coffeehouse, where you can "hang," read the paper, or have a casual business meeting. The menu consists of light, healthy fare with salads, sandwiches, fresh-baked breads, cheeses, and, of course, coffee. Henry's is the brainchild of Gibson Guitar head Henry Juszkiewicz, so it's not surprising that there is an incredible sound system in place for the eclectic mix of entertainment.

The serenity inside **Ichiban** (109 Second Ave. N., 615-254-7185; $$, ☐) masks the cacophony going on outside. *Sushi, tempura, sukiyaki*, and other traditional Japanese dishes are available at the two-story dining spot.

Take a taste of the world down under at **Laurell's 2nd Avenue Oyster Bar and Grill** (123 Second Ave. N., 615-244-1230; $$, ☐). Since 1985, this cozy seafood haunt has been serving up po'boys, crab cakes, barbecued shrimp, and other underwater delights.

Market Street Brewery and Public House (134 Second Ave. N., 615-259-9611; $$, ☐) was the first in Nashville to combine hand-crafted beer and food. A variety of microbrews are on tap at Market Street, all wonderful paired with Cajun dishes, sandwiches, and grilled items. The turn-of-the-century setting with its rich woodwork is a pretty place to dine. Head to the far back and you can catch a glimpse of the river.

There was a time when fondue was *très chic*. Even though some may think it went the way of avocado green appliances, you can still fondue your dinner at **The Melting Pot** (166 Second Ave. N., 615-742-4970; $$–$$$, ☐). Simmer and dip morsels of chicken, beef, and seafood into hot liquids such as cheese, broth, and peanut oil, and then finish with fruit and cake dipped into warm chocolate.

The historic building that houses **Merchants Restaurant** (401 Broadway, 615-254-1892; $$–$$$, ☐) is full of history, some of which can be seen on the walls of the three-story dining spot (like the letter from a Union soldier to his fiancée). The structure once served as a house of ill-repute and barely missed the wrecking ball before being restored in the late '80s. The opening of the Merchants started also the trend of preserving Downtown's older buildings. Food here ranges from grilled seafood to innovative pasta dishes and is popular among the power-lunch folks. There's a pleasant bar on the lower level and tables for outdoor dining.

Mere Bulles (152 Second Ave. N., 615-256-1946; $$–$$$, ☐), or "Mother Bubbles," is a cavernous restaurant that draws people for the food and entertainment (see "Nightlife"). The menu boasts some interesting combinations with steak, seafood, and poultry, but occasionally the dishes don't live up to their billing. Wednesday evenings the restaurant stages wine tastings with complimentary appetizers. This is the building where Maxwell House coffee, named after the city's original Maxwell House Hotel, was blended in the late 1800s.

The Old Spaghetti Factory (160 Second Ave. N., 615-254-9010; $–$$, ☐) opened its doors on Second Avenue before the area became such a thriving tourist district. It has continued by serving up reasonably priced pasta dishes, including spaghetti with a choice of sauces, that come with a salad, a beverage, spumoni ice cream, and all-you-can-eat bread.

Another sign of Nashville's downtown resurgence occurred when **Planet Hollywood** (324 Broadway; $$, ☐) announced it was opening a branch in Music City. Diners will find fresh fish, grilled meats, salads, pastas, and pizza at the restaurant, which is famous for its movie star investors Bruce Willis, Demi Moore, Sylvester Stallone, and Arnold Schwarzenegger (his mother's apple strudel is on the menu). Movie memorabilia and a handprint wall of famous film and television stars set the eatery apart, as well as the preview trailers of soon-to-be-released movies. There's also a full line of Planet Hollywood clothing sold at this worldwide chain.

Some people get a kick out of going to a restaurant and cooking their own dinner; some prefer to be pampered when dining out. At the **Prime Cut Steakhouse** (170 Second Ave. N., 615-242-3083; $$$, ☐), you can do either—grill your own steak, chicken, or seafood, or let the chef take charge. Dinners include salad, baked potato, and all the Texas toast you can eat.

San Antonio Grill (208 Commerce St. 259-4413; $, ☐) (better known as San Antonio Taco Co.) is a great place to grab a soft taco, some chips and salsa, or an enchilada plate. It's cheap and a better alternative than typical fast food. Plus, the brick and turquoise dining room offers a casual and comfortable atmosphere.

Schlotzsky's Deli (222 Second Ave. N. in the Washington Square building, 615-259-3777; $) has fast become a popular spot for sandwiches, pizzas, soups, salads, and desserts. Bite into a turkey and bacon club or opt for the onion and mushroom pizza. There are also Kid Schlotzsky's for the little ones.

Windows on the Cumberland (112 Second Ave. N., 615-251-0097; $–$$) is appropriately named for the large windows that look out over the river. For years, Windows has served health-conscious fare, from steamed vegetables to smoked turkey sandwiches and vegetarian chili. Often live music provides additional ambiance to this Market Street Emporium eatery.

Wolfy's (425 Broadway, 615-251-1621; $–$$, □), a dive of a place, turns out good deli sandwiches and sports items borrowed from Gerst House in East Nashville, which used to be owned by the same proprietor. Bavarian pizza (sausage and cheese layered on marble rye), oyster rolls, *schnitzel*, and sausages pack the flavor, but you can't go wrong with a cheeseburger and seasoned curly fries. There is live music nightly (with a cover charge) that varies from blues to bluegrass, all played against an amusing Bavarian backdrop.

NIGHTLIFE

A number of restaurants in The District feature live entertainment, plus there are several good stops in the revitalized Printers Alley. It's best to call ahead to find out who's playing and to inquire about cover charges.

The Ace of Clubs (114 Second Ave. S., 615-254-ACES) is known as a great place to dance. There's a mix of live music and DJs, with an emphasis on rock. Go-Go Mania takes place weekend nights, with go-go dancers doing their thing in the club's cages.

Barbara's (207 Printers Alley, 615-259-2272) is an Alley favorite and features both well-known and aspiring local artists. And there's always a good house band to get things rolling.

If you're looking for blues, head to **Bourbon Street Blues and Boogie Bar** (220 Printers Alley, 615-242-5837). A seven-piece house band backs up musicians from as far away as Chicago and New Orleans. Every Tuesday is Mardi Gras, which means foot-stomping music, decorations, special drinks, and a chance to spin the *lagniappe* wheel for gifts and prizes. Menu items include red beans and rice, gumbo, and crawfish.

On the lower level of Mere Bulles restaurant is **Club Mere Bulles** (152 Second Ave. N., 615-256-CLUB), where you can hear Top 40, live jazz, and piano tunes. The bar is a popular hangout for both tourists and area residents.

There's both food and entertainment in the **Music City Mix Factory** (300 Second Ave. S., 615-251-8899 or 248-2233), a converted multilevel warehouse building. The structure houses **The Zoo,** a haven for rock-and-rollers; the **French Market Cafe,** serving up New Orleans–style fare; **Close Encounters,** a Top 40 dance club; and **The Planetarium,** a rooftop cabana with food and drinks. There's even occasional amateur boxing at Music City Mix Factory.

Robert's Western Wear (416 Broadway, 615-256-7937) became the place to go when the band BR5-49 (named for a *Hee Haw* routine) captured everybody's attention in 1995. If you're lucky, you can still see the rockabilly group there (although a record contract often has them on the road) as well as other country artists, and you might even take to the dance floor—or buy a pair of boots.

Skull's Rainbow Room (222 Printers Alley, 615-251-9076) may be one of the few remaining honky-tonks left over from the Alley's heyday after the war. Stars like Willie Nelson, Johnny Cash, Hank Williams, Sr., and Dottie West played Skull's in the early days, and many of their pictures line the club's walls. Today some of country's newest stars perform in the Rainbow Room, which is open six days a week.

Over the years, patrons of **Tootsie's Orchid Lounge** (422 Broadway, 615-726-0463), named for proprietress Tootsie Bess, have seen the best-loved country stars perform there, especially when the Grand Ole Opry was broadcast from the Ryman Auditorium just around the corner. The Orchid's purple exterior makes it easy to spot, and there's always some country singer belting out tunes on the small stage.

At the **Wildhorse Saloon** (120 Second Ave. N., 615-256-WILD or 251-1000), you can line dance, be part of a TNN taping, eat lunch or dinner, and even take free dance lessons. This Gaylord Entertainment Co. project also features concerts, live shows, and other special events. The 3,300-square-foot dance floor and its large-screen TVs give dancers plenty of room to kick up their heels. Or watch the action from the upstairs restaurant while munching a burger or barbecue.

DOWNTOWN

Even though The District has seen the most fervent growth, that's not to say the rest of downtown hasn't also expanded. The reopening of the Ryman Auditorium (see "Local Treasures" in this section), the restoration of the Cummins Station warehouses, and the multimillion-dollar renovation of the Hermitage Hotel have all brought significant changes to the Downtown section of the city. The new arena on Broadway and the stadium proposed for the east bank of the Cumberland River are sure to give even more impetus for growth here.

The Nashville skyline is made distinctive by the South Central Bell building—otherwise known as the "Batman Building"—the bullet-shaped First Union Tower, the postmodern SunTrust Bank structure, and one of the city's first skyscrapers, the L & C Tower. The American General building comes to life each evening, when a different message is revealed by the combination of lights and closed window blinds.

The Nashville Convention & Visitors Bureau has a Tourist Information Center open daily at the foot of Victory Memorial Bridge on the east side of the Cumberland River (615-259-4747). It will be replaced by a visitors bureau located inside the Nashville Arena tower.

ATTRACTIONS

There are a lot more than books at the **Ben West Public Library** (225 Polk Ave., 615-862-5800; free). For example, the Nashville Room on the second floor specializes in local history/genealogy (615-862-5782). It's right next door to **WPLN radio,** the city's public radio station (615-862-5810). Kids won't want to miss the **Paint-the-Town Puppet Players** (formerly the Tom Tichenor Marionette Troupe). Already well known for his hand puppets and storytelling, Tichenor founded the troupe at the public library in 1938. All of the marionettes used in the performances (which are free) as well as the background scenery were handmade by the talented puppeteer, who was with the library for 50 years before his retirement in 1988. Even though Tichenor died in 1992, children can still delight in his whimsical characters during the plays held on Thursday mornings and the first and third Saturdays of each month.

Historic Nashville (P.O. Box 190516, 615-244-7835; admission fee) conducts walking tours of downtown that include sites like the Ryman

LOCAL TREASURES: RYMAN AUDITORIUM

For more than 100 years, the Ryman Auditorium has been a place to see the movers and shakers of the entertainment industry and well-known voices from the political ranks. Its halls have been filled with prominent names like Charlie Chaplin, Katharine Hepburn, W. C. Fields, Sarah Bernhardt, Helen Keller, Harpo Marx, Mae West, and Enrico Caruso. Lectures, political rallies, and ballet performances have also been staged there.

Today, after an $8.5 million renovation completed in 1994, voices of those with stature still ring out in the "Carnegie Hall of the South." Bluegrass fans can hear Bill Monroe or Alison Krauss, Ricky Skaggs, and Doc Watson. Gospel greats, jazz artists, classical musicians, and songwriters take to the stage, too, in addition to performances like *Always . . . Patsy Cline,* a musical detailing the legendary star's life that drew large crowds in 1994 and 1995.

When the Ryman was first built in 1892 by Nashville riverboat captain Thomas Ryman, it was known as the Union Gospel Tabernacle. Ryman "got religion" after being converted by colorful evangelist Sam Jones. A history of religious revivals and the beginning of the Grand Ole Opry radio show there in 1943 later gave it the moniker "The Mother Church of Country Music." The Grand Ole Opry, the longest running radio show in the world, made its home here until 1974, and then the auditorium was essentially closed for 20 years.

By day now, the Ryman is open for touring. Visitors are greeted by life-size bronze statues of Opry greats Minnie Pearl and Roy Acuff done by Bell Buckle, Tennessee artist Russell Faxon. Guests can relive some of the early days with memorabilia and photographs of Opry stars, interactive videos narrated by country greats like Johnny Cash, Vince Gill, and Little Jimmy Dickens, programs and showprints from various productions that took place here, and a large mural of the Opry cast when it broadcast from the Ryman. The original oak pews have been restored for seating, and the walls feature oil paintings of the building itself and its transformation from 1892 to 1994. The souvenir shop even allows you to take home some memories.

The Ryman, located at 116 Fifth Avenue North, is open daily for self-guided tours for a nominal fee (615-254-1445). Information about the calendar of shows and tickets call be obtained by calling (615) 889-6611.

Auditorium, the Arcade, and The District. Tours are available April through October by reservation only and begin at Fort Nashborough.

Tucked into the back of the **Tennessee Arts Commission** offices is a small gallery (404 James Robertson Pkwy., 615-741-1701; free) devoted to showing the work of Tennessee artists. Rotating shows are offered throughout the year and range from folk art to sculpture and paintings.

It's hard to miss the **Tennessee State Capitol** (Charlotte Ave., between Sixth and Seventh Aves., 615-741-1621; free), as it stands on the highest hill of the central city. The structure was designed by architect William Strickland and is regarded as one of the best Greek Revival–style buildings in the country. Although many interior areas have been restored, the exterior of the capitol looks much as it did when it was completed in 1859. Interestingly, Strickland died before the structure was finished and according to his wishes is buried in a wall near the north entrance. The tomb of President and Mrs. James K. Polk stands on the eastern slope of the grounds, as does a bronze equestrian statue of President Andrew Jackson that was unveiled during the Nashville Centennial in 1880. Guided tours of the structure are offered during the week, or you can pick up a brochure and take your own tour through the hallowed halls. Reservations for large groups are recommended and can be made by calling (615) 741-0830.

The **Tennessee State Museum** (505 Deaderick St., 615-741-2692; free except for occasional temporary exhibits) is located in the bottom of the James K. Polk Building, which is better known as the Tennessee Performing Arts Center. The museum chronicles the state's history, and items range from Indian artifacts to early Tennessee portraits to silver and quilts. There are items relating to Tennessee's three presidents—Andrew Jackson, James K. Polk, and Andrew Johnson—in addition to full-scale replicas of period rooms and buildings. The state museum also hosts a wide array of traveling exhibitions that showcase local artwork as well as that of international status. **The Military Museum,** a branch of the TSM, operates in the War Memorial Building across the street and houses exhibits detailing America's role in conflicts from the Spanish-American War to World War II. Memorials to Tennessee's soldiers are found on the plaza area surrounding the building.

SHOPPING

Associated Salvage Co. (121 Third Ave. S., 615-255-2707) really doesn't sell salvage at all these days, but the store did when it first opened. It's now a window treatment store, with discount draperies, blinds, shades, fabrics, and drapery rods. The shop sells custom-made bed-spreads and offers a quilting service.

Three levels of stores await shoppers at **Church Street Centre** (625 Church St., 615-256-6644). The Limited, Victoria's Secret, Walden-books, Impostors, and some 45 other businesses are housed here. The **Nashville Arts Gallery** (615-256-7333), located on the third floor, presents rotating local and regional art exhibits as well as crafts by Tennessee artists. **Imagine Gallery** (615-320-5670 or 254-3102) is the place to find limited-edition artwork by musical greats like John Lennon (hence the name), Miles Davis, Jerry Garcia, and Rolling Stones guitarist Ron Wood. The store also has a limited selection of T-shirts. The center's food court is a popular stop for downtown employees to grab lunch or a snack, and you can get two hours of free parking in the Church Street Centre garage.

The Nashville Arcade (225 Fourth Ave. N.) offers a unique shop-ping/dining experience. This block-long area, between Union and Church streets and Fourth and Fifth avenues north, was inspired by a mall in Milan, Italy. Built in 1903, The Arcade contains an interesting assortment of eateries and stores under an iron and glass roof. Arcades were once more common in downtowns across America, but now only four structures of this type exist in this country. Varallo's Too, Calypso Cafe, The Greek Touch, and Maggie's Cafe are a few of the restaurants located here. Shops include The Tennessee Coffee Co., The Peanut Shop, and the Purple Opossum card and gift shop, plus there are offices, a post office, a beauty shop, and a fruit stand.

The Salvage Store (119 Third Ave. S., 615-242-8473) is known by locals as the place to shop for discount fabric, upholstery supplies, slipcovers, and area rugs (including Orientals). It started in 1952 as one store with Associated Salvage Co. The two divided in the 1970s with separate owners, but they still complement one another.

DINING

Capitol Grille (231 Sixth Ave. N. in the Hermitage Suite Hotel, 615-244-3121, ext. 116; $$–$$$, □) made a big name for itself within a short time after opening. Chef Guillermo Thomas breaks interesting ground with his innovative entrees, which lend a regional twist to New American cuisine. This cozy dining spot with its arched ceilings and dark wood was named one of *Esquire* magazine's best new restaurants of 1995, and it's a billing the eatery is living up to. Dishes like a fried green tomato salad with feta and wild boar bacon, soft-shell crawfish with eggplant and honey-roasted nuts, fresh corn polenta with portabella mushrooms and roasted garlic, and other intriguing combinations are hard to beat. Desserts show the same panache, with choices like banana-rum cheesecake, crème brûlée

Napoleon, and warm chocolate cake. Try the Capitol Grille for lunch or Sunday brunch, too.

Demos' Steak and Spaghetti House (300 Commerce St., 615-256-4655; $–$$, ☐) is always bustling with people who like to hoist their forks with bites of steak, pasta, chicken, and seafood. Try the K.C. strip for a satisfying cut of beef or dig into some seafood fettuccine for a taste of lighter fare. Low cholesterol and vegetarian selections are available, too.

Koto Japanese Restaurant (137 Seventh Ave. N., 615-255-8122; $$, ☐) started out as a small hole in the wall on Fourth Avenue South and was one of the city's first sushi bars when it opened in 1985. Fortunately its move to a larger location in 1994 didn't affect the friendly service and well-prepared food. A few of the sushi selections are named for regular customers (the Wayne roll, the Norro roll), and Koto also serves other delicious Japanese fare like *sashimi, tempura, miso* soup, and *soba*.

If you're in the mood for steak, head to **Morton's of Chicago** (641 Church St., 615-259-4558; $$$, ☐), which has a reputation nationwide for its generous portions of beef. The restaurant also serves swordfish, salmon, live Maine lobsters, shrimp, and even chicken. The clubby downtown location is popular for business dinners and anniversary celebrations, and Morton's also stages occasional cigar smokers.

Just off Second Avenue is **Royal Thai** (204 Commerce St., 615-256-0312; $$, ☐), where you can find well-prepared entrees that reward the taste buds with a melding of flavors, textures, and colors. *Satays*, soups, curries, seafood, and the omnipresent *pad Thai* (found on street corners in the Southeast Asian country) grace the menu. The restaurant even entices locals to wade through the tourists to get here.

Satsuma Tea Room (417 Union St., 615-256-0760; $) has been serving generations of Nashvillians with lunchroom specials ranging from chicken à la king to corned beef and cabbage since 1918. The "men's table" (though women sit there now, too) at the eatery is notorious for drawing legislators, attorneys, and other professionals to its chairs, where the issues of the day are discussed over congealed salad, fresh-baked rolls, and spice tea.

The folks that own **Sole Mio** (94 Peabody St., 615-256-4013; $$, ☐) also have a restaurant in Italy, so obviously they know their stuff. The dishes of Northern Italy are specialties at Sole Mio, as well as thin-crust pizza, homemade pasta dishes, veal, and fish creations. The outdoor patio and windowed dining room give patrons a pleasant view of downtown.

The **Stock-Yard Restaurant** (901 Second Ave. N. and Stockyard Blvd., 615-255-6464; $$–$$$, ☐) boasts "Sizzlin' Steaks and Sizzlin' Stars," referring to both the dining room and the well-known

Bullpen lounge. Tourists, in particular, are drawn to the Stock-Yard for its gargantuan portions of beef and seafood served in a historic setting where Nashville's old stockyards used to be. The lounge is a popular spot for dancing, with live entertainment nightly. There is also a Sunday buffet, and private dining rooms are available.

Varallo's (817 Church St., 615-256-9109; $) is a real part of Nashville's history and claims to be the oldest restaurant in the city. It has been passed down through generations of Varallos since it opened in 1907 (with several locations). But since 1949, diners can find it at the corner of Ninth Avenue North and Church Street. Chili (order a bowl of three-way), meat-and-three offerings, and home-made desserts (lay claim to rice pudding at the start of your meal) draw folks into the modest urban setting. More of the same is on tap at Varallo's Too in The Nashville Arcade.

NIGHTLIFE

3rd & Lindsley Bar and Grill (818 Third Ave. S., 615-259-9891) features live blues and R&B nightly. It seems a bit incongruous in the small strip center where it's located, but that doesn't affect the vibes produced there. The Wooten Brothers, Tracy Nelson, Jonell Mosser and Enough Rope, and Mike Griffin and The Unknown Blues Band are some of the talent that takes the stage. The bar/grill adds a menu of quesadillas, burgers, barbecue, and shrimp kabobs (also available for take-out).

328 Performance Hall (328 Fourth Ave. S., 615-259-3288) is known for shows that feature cutting-edge performers as well as familiar songsters. Robert Cray, Janis Ian, Collective Soul, Shawn Colvin, and Filter are just a sampling of the music that echoes from 328. Johnny Jackson's Soul Satisfaction gets the joint hoppin' on Friday and Saturday nights, and the venue is often used for special benefits and other citywide events.

ACCOMMODATIONS

Crowne Plaza Nashville (623 Union St., 615-259-2000 or 800-HOLI-DAY; $$–$$$, ☐) is distinguished by its revolving rooftop restaurant called The Pinnacle. Of the nearly 500 rooms in this Holiday Inn property, many have a panoramic view of downtown. Crowne Plaza is also close to the Tennessee State Capitol and has an indoor pool, a fitness center, meeting rooms, and a coffee shop.

More than 300 rooms, including 26 suites, are available in the downtown **Doubletree Hotel** (315 Fourth Ave. N., 615-244-8200 or 800-528-0444; $$–$$$, ☐). Opt for one of the glass-walled corner rooms for a better view in this angular high-rise, which was renovated in 1995. The Plaza Cafe serves three meals a day, and there are meeting rooms, a lounge, an indoor pool, an exercise room, and a sauna.

After undergoing a $3.5 million restoration, the **Hermitage Suite Hotel** (231 Sixth Ave. N., 615-244-3121 or 800-251-1908; $$–$$$, □) emerged with newly redone suites, a sumptuous lobby, and an award-winning restaurant called Capitol Grille (see "Dining"). Built in 1910, the Hermitage is an elegant Beaux Arts–style hotel that once served as headquarters for suffragist and antisuffragist groups. It is listed on the National Register of Historic Places and has hosted six U.S. presidents. The Hermitage also became home to famous pool player Minnesota Fats for awhile. There are 120 suites in the 10-story hotel, meeting rooms, and two lounges—the Verandah and the Historic Oak Bar—plus the green-and-black marble men's restroom is no doubt the city's coolest.

The Renaissance Nashville Hotel (611 Commerce St., 615-255-8400 or 800-HOTELS-1; $$–$$$, □), formerly known as The Stouffer, is always busy. That's because it's attached to the Nashville Convention Center and the three-level Church Street Centre shopping mall. Almost 700 rooms are offered and quickly fill up with conventioneers. There are weekend packages, a fitness center, Commerce Street Bar and Grill, the Bridge Bar & Deli (located in the breezeway between the hotel and the Church Street Centre), an indoor pool, an exercise room, a sun deck, and 24-hour room service. Two upper floors provide additional amenities like private access, turndown service, express check-out, complimentary breakfast, hors d'oeuvres in the lounge, and the best views of downtown.

EAST NASHVILLE

The many historic neighborhoods located across the Cumberland River have been gentrified in the past 20 years. Areas like Lockeland Springs, Edgefield, and East End have come to life with the restoration of elegant Victorian homes, bungalows, and Italianate-style residences. Edgefield, which is one of Nashville's oldest suburbs, became the city's first locally zoned historic district in 1978 and contains a large concentration of Victorian homes. It was also the site of the city's worst fire disaster in 1916, which devastated large tracts of the neighborhood.

The east bank of the Cumberland River has been pegged for the city's new 65,000-seat football stadium, which will surely change the dynamics of this historic area, bringing in more development and traffic. It's scheduled to be completed by 1998.

ATTRACTIONS

The **Shelby Bottoms Greenway** (next to Shelby Park, 615-862-8400; free) is an area of 810 acres on the Cumberland River undergoing development. This is a place to observe nature, take a walk, or even meditate. Shelby Bottoms was privately owned for years as farmland until the city began purchasing it in 1994. It might feel like you're miles from civilization, but you're smack dab in the middle of it. Paved trails, mulched trails, open fields, interpretive signage, and an observation deck attracts those who enjoy the outdoors. Bring some binoculars to get a look at some of the waterfowl that hang out here.

DINING

The Gerst Haus (228 Woodland St., 615-256-9760; $$, ☐) has been the place to congregate for politicians, journalists, and other down-town upstarts since it originally opened in 1952. Besides large mugs of beer, patrons order up oyster rolls, Bavarian pizza, knockwurst, sausages, and smoked pork loin in the boisterous beer hall, which has been located in East Nashville since 1970. There is a live polka band on weekends (with a cover charge) that makes the experience even more authentic and fun.

East Nashvillians (and those who reside across the river) flock to the **Radio Cafe** (1313 Woodland St., 615-262-1766; $) for coffee, bagels, muffins, pastries, sandwiches, soup, and conversation. There is music in the evenings, and the place is decorated with antique pharmacy cabinets from Hoosiers Pharmacy, which occupied the site for 85 years. Radio Cafe also sells crafts and other artwork as well as bulk coffee beans.

GULCH

The Gulch area is dominated by Union Station and the adjoining shed, which served as the city's train station for 79 years. The future of the iron and steel shed has been debated for years, all the while falling into further disrepair (some are hoping for it to become a new city library). Its extraordinary truss system earned the shed status as a National Historic Landmark along with the station itself. With the opening of Cummins Station (the renovated warehouses at 10th Avenue South and Demonbreun), the district has become more accessible and popular for shopping, dining, and nightlife. The city's newspaper offices are also situated in the Gulch, with both the *Tennesseean* and the *Nashville Banner* housed in the same structure at 1100 Broadway.

SHOPPING

Surroundings (209 10th Ave. S., 615-726-4004) is one of those stores that makes you crazy with desire. There are beautiful futons, mirrors, hand-painted chairs, frames, lamps, linens, and other decorative accessories for the home. Surroundings also has many one-of-a-kind items by furniture makers and other craftspeople.

If you're into used clothing, **Wardrobe Recyclers Ltd.** (209 10th Ave. S., 615-251-8959) is the place to find a good array of well-taken-care-of apparel for both men and women.

Zeitgeist (209 10th Ave. S., 615-256-4805) does as its name suggests by presenting a rotating schedule of the best in contemporary art with shows by both local and national artists. The gallery often shows the artists' processes as well as the final products and invites them to speak to audiences about their work. The concrete floors and changing colored walls provide a hip venue for showing work. The gallery also carries contemporary lighting and some furniture.

DINING

Arthur's (1001 Broadway in Union Station, 615-255-1494; $$$, ☐) treats diners to continental food in an elegant and romantic atmosphere off the lobby of the Union Station. The award-winning dining spot is known for its spoken menu and *prix fixe* meals of seafood, beef, lamb, poultry, and occasional game. Tournedos of beef, salmon with lobster mousse, and veal scaloppine are indicative of some of the choices, which change daily. The soaring ceilings and stained-glass windows add to the ambiance, making Arthur's a favorite for special celebrations and business for more than 15 years. Bananas Foster and Café Diablo are standards in the restaurant's repertoire, as are the martinis—distinguished by a Stilton cheese–stuffed olive.

"Steaks, Chops, and Pasta with a Regional Twist" is how **Cafe One Two Three** (123 12th Ave. N., 615-255-2233; $$–$$$, ☐) bills itself. This is the more upscale of the three Jody Faison restaurants that lie in the same block. Entrees like chili grilled salmon, grilled peanut-crusted pork chops, and collard green fettuccine show the chef's deft skill in combining ingredients. Delicious accompaniments—red pepper "hi-d-ho" cakes, pecan popcorn rice pilaf, and cheese jalapeño grits—add their own inventive flair to the meal. Add to that the urban decor, attractive wooden bar (serving 'til the wee hours), and tunes by crooners like Frank Sinatra and Tony Bennett, and Cafe One Two Three hits all the high notes.

The revamped warehouse space of **Jules Dining Hall and Bar Car** (209 10th Ave. S., 615-259-4875; $–$$, ☐) complements the creative dishes this eatery churns out. Interesting tapas offerings, salads, sandwiches, entrees, and vegetarian recipes pair old standards with new spices, sauces, and salsas. A great way to begin is with the Bruschetta Classico, a large serving of grilled eggplant, roasted elephant garlic, yellow bell peppers, feta, capers, and sun-dried tomato Montrachet. Then try the lime chicken with black bean sauce, grilled pepper-turkey Reuben "cranwich," or the Buddha Bowl of rice, beans, tofu, steamed kale, and "Gulch gravy." There are pool tables and another bar in the back room.

The Pie Wagon (118 12th Ave. S., 615-256-5893; $) originated in 1923, and although it has changed hands a few times, diners can still find spicy fried chicken, catfish, pork tenderloin, pork chops, real mashed potatoes (plus more than a dozen other vegetables), and a fresh cobbler and pudding each day. Early risers head here for standard breakfast fare, too.

12th & Porter (114 12th Ave. N., 615-254-7236; $–$$, ☐) is yet another Faison-owned restaurant located on this short block. The distinctive turquoise-and-black exterior make this dining spot hard to miss, and the funkiness continues inside. Standards include Pasta YaYa (sausage and chicken in a Cajun cream sauce), Black & Blue Plate Special (blackened shrimp, red sauce, and blue cheese over fettuccine), and other creative sandwiches, pizzas, and calzones. In the evenings the Playroom hosts some of the best local and national musicians and always draws a big crowd.

NIGHTLIFE

The Pub of Love (123 12th Ave. N., 615-256-LOVE) is decorated in early yard-sale style, as evidenced by the stage, which was crafted from the bed of a 1959 Ford pickup. Pool tables, darts, and video games accent the live music, beer, and food items (most of which are catered out of neighboring 12th & Porter and Cafe One Two Three). The facility is often used for private parties.

The building may be modest, but the music that reverberates from **The Station Inn** (402 12th Ave. S., 615-255-3307) is anything but. The small music venue is the place to see the best in bluegrass while munching on pizza, nachos, and hot dogs. The Station Inn opened in 1974 and features talents ranging from Bill Monroe to the Nashville Bluegrass Band and the Fairfield Four.

ACCOMMODATIONS

You can't catch a train there anymore, but you can still envision what the historic **Union Station** (1001 Broadway, 615-726-1001 or 800-331-2123; $$–$$$, ☐) was like when it was a bustling terminal. The Romanesque limestone structure was built in 1900 by the L&N Railroad and is one of the country's last surviving turn-of-the-century railroad stations. Its clock tower makes it one of the most visible landmarks in the city. After years of neglect, Union Station reopened 1986 as luxury hotel and is now part of the Grand Heritage chain of accommodations. The domed lobby area is worth a visit just to see its gilded plasterwork, 65-foot stained-glass ceiling, and other ornate detail work. There are approximately 124 rooms, all decorated differently, and 11 suites. Arthur's restaurant (see "Dining") is tucked into one corner, and the Broadway Bistro is the hotel's casual dining area, with soups, salads, and sandwiches on the menu.

EIGHTH AVENUE/ FRANKLIN ROAD

There's a wide variety of businesses located off of Eighth Avenue South, which later turns into Franklin Road and leads to Brentwood and eventually Franklin, Tennessee. The area is home to Greer Stadium (of guitar-shaped scoreboard fame), where the Nashville Sounds play baseball, and to the Tennessee State Fairgrounds, the place for the annual state fair each September and a slew of other events throughout the year. The latter include the huge monthly flea market (the fourth weekend of every month except during December, when it's the third weekend), which boasts more than 1,000 dealers and is considered one of the Top 10 flea markets in the country (615-862-5016).

ATTRACTIONS

The kids will wake up to the wonder of science at the **Cumberland Science Museum** (800 Ft. Negley Blvd., 615-862-5160; admission fee), which started in 1944 as the Nashville Children's Museum. See a hot-air balloon rise, discover secrets about the human body, and watch a metal ball take a roller-coaster ride through the Kinetic Coaster. In addition, there are places to climb, an old-fashioned store to play in, a Japanese room to visit, and see-and-touch animal shows. The museum, which was built and opened in 1973, and Sudekum Planetarium display rotating exhibits as well, and special events are planned throughout the year. The museum shop has an unusual array of games, books, jewelry, and other science-oriented toys.

If you want to see how the other half lives, visit the beautiful **Governor's Residence** (882 S. Curtiswood Ln., 615-383-5401; free), which was built as private home in 1929. The 26-room structure was bought by the state in 1948 and has served as the home for Tennessee's chief executive since then. Located on 10 acres in a quiet residential area with a terrific view of the Nashville hills, free guided tours of the 15,000-square-foot home are conducted on Tuesdays and Thursdays by reservation. Visitors can see the home's first level and exterior, and docents provide interesting historical tidbits.

On the grounds of the Ellington Agricultural Center is the **Oscar L. Farris Agricultural Museum** (440 Hogan Rd., 615-360-0197; free).

Housed in a large, renovated horse barn and run by the state, the museum holds a blacksmith shop, more than 2,500 farm implements and rural household items from the 1800s and early 1900s, and the Tennessee Agricultural Hall of Fame. Year-round programs introduce children to old-fashioned button games, folk stories, and how to make corn shuck dolls in addition to sessions on pioneers and Native Americans. Adults can also take classes to learn 19th-century crafts like basket weaving and quilting. The museum stages two festivals each year—the Historic Rural Life Festival and the Music & Molasses Festival (see "Festivals").

Some 23,000 graves dot the **Nashville City Cemetery** (1001 Fourth Ave. S.; free), which opened in 1822. This is Nashville's oldest remaining public cemetery and one of the few in Tennessee listed in the National Register of Historic Places. Several prominent people are buried there, including Nashville city founder General James Robertson, original Fisk Jubilee singers Mable Lewis Imes and Ella Sheppard Moore, and Captain William Driver, who gave the name "Old Glory" to the American flag. An act of Congress allows the flag to fly at his grave 24 hours a day. A brochure available at the Metro Historical Commission can guide you through the cemetery.

Travellers Rest (636 Farrell Pkwy., 615-832-2962; admission fee) was the home of John Overton, who was a close friend and law partner of Andrew Jackson. He was also a state Supreme Court jurist, and he co-founded the city of Memphis. Overton's home, which was begun in 1799, served as headquarters for Confederate General John B. Hood before the Battle of Nashville in 1864. The residence began as a two-story Federal-style house, but additions in 1812, 1828, and 1887 show varying architectural styles.

Travellers Rest remained in the Overton family until 1948, then was given by its last owner—the Nashville Railroad Company—to the Colonial Dames of America in Tennessee to be managed as a historic site. It is currently used as an interpretive farm of the early 19th century. The home holds the largest public collection of early Tennessee-made furniture, and visitors enjoy the restored outbuildings and gardens. The gift shop features regional specialties and old-fashioned toys, and several special celebrations take place annually (see "Festivals").

SHOPPING

There is a stretch of Eighth Avenue between Wedgewood Avenue and Craighead Street that brims with antique stores. Almost a dozen shops specialize in furnishings, knickknacks, jewelry, china, and linens, including one—the Art Deco Shoppe and Antiques—with a terrific selection of period items. A few other stores are situated on nearby Wedgewood Avenue, too, dealing mainly in curios.

For flowers at a wholesale prices, check out **Smith & Rogers** (701 Craighead St., 615-297-4000). Shoppers here can find fresh cut flowers, candles, seasonal decorations, silk flowers, crystal, brass, and a wide assortment of gift items. There's even coffee beans and furniture, too.

DINING

If it's meat-and-three you're craving, head to **Arnold's Country Kitchen** (605 Eighth Ave. S., 615-256-4455; $). Here you can select from fried chicken, catfish, carved round of beef, country steak, and a whole slew of vegetables, including the elusive fried green tomatoes. Try the chocolate pie or blackberry cobbler to top your meal. Breakfast brings on scratch biscuits, eggs, sausage, country ham, and a good cup of joe.

When Gardner "Hap" Townes started his restaurant in 1921, he knew the kind of plate lunch people wanted. It can still be found today (although Hap has died and the younger "Hap" retired) at **Hap Townes Restaurant** (493 Humphreys St., 615-242-7035, $). Head through the line for beef tips and noodles, fried chicken, hamburger steaks, creamed potatoes, turnip greens, macaroni and cheese, deviled eggs, and the legendary stewed raisins. There's usually a fresh cobbler to satisfy your sweet tooth, too, in this distinctive stone diner.

NIGHTLIFE

Inside the cavernous space of **The Cannery** (1 Cannery Row, off Eighth Ave. S., 615-251-0979; concert hotline 615-780-3567), visitors can experience concerts, art shows, television/video productions, and music. Most evenings find a variety of bands entertaining customers, in addition to other special events scheduled periodically. The Local Motive Music Store, open afternoons, specializes in music by local bands, T-shirts, used compact discs and tapes, bohemian clothing, and jewelry.

Douglas Corner Cafe (2106-A Eighth Ave. S., 615-298-1688) has made a name for itself by serving up fine entertainment and good victuals. Cheeseburgers on French bread and Cajun chicken sandwiches can quell food desires while you listen to the music, ranging from pop to tunes by local songwriters. There are usually two shows a night, six days a week.

You can hear blues, jazz, country, and rock acts at **The Sutler** (2608 Franklin Rd., 615-297-9195). Both local and national bands and artists take to the stage in this rustic, Western-style music club. In daylight hours, The Sutler is a popular place for burgers, sandwiches, and plate lunches.

If you want someone to tickle your funny bone, take in a show at **Zanies Comedy Showplace** (2025 Eighth Ave. S., 615-269-0221), where comedians take to the stage nightly. Nationally known comics as well as those known regionally headline here, including names like Robert Klein and Killer Beaz. Open-mike nights are also part of the act at Zanies, which has been in business since 1983. Some early shows are smoke-free, and tickets are available at Zanies or through Ticketmaster (615-737-4849).

ELLISTON PLACE

While this strip of establishments might be familiar to Vanderbilt University students or those employed at Baptist Hospital, for newcomers it's a bit off the beaten path. The small street is tucked off of West End Avenue and leads into Church Street.

The Elliston Place area offers a mix of retail and restaurants, with everything from rare books to unusual gifts. The strip is sure to draw even more people with the opening of the Hampton Inn.

SHOPPING

Elder's Book Store (2115 Elliston Pl., 615-327-1867) is not your typical bookseller. This dusty shop specializes in collectible/rare titles, although they do stock new books, too. Browsers interested in the Civil War, Southern history, literature, or culture will find a wide selection here.

Across the street is **Mosko's** (2204 Elliston Pl., 615-327-2658), which has made its home here since 1977. "Eat it, Read It, Smoke It" has remained the newsstand's motto because you can get food, magazines, and cigars here. The store has a huge selection of cards and out-of-town newspapers, and boasts a walk-in humidor and numerous eccentric gifts—besides making some of the best sandwiches in the city (see "Dining").

Farther up the block, shoppers will want to browse in **Street Smart** (2416 Elliston Pl., 615-329-9337) for practical and functional European imported pottery and other unusual gifts. Savor a wedge of almond cheesecake or chocolate raspberry torte (served on the pottery, of course) with coffee while you check out all the unique items.

DINING

Cafe Elliston (210 Louise Ave., 615-329-0024; $, ☐) is a cozy house-turned-restaurant where you can sip a cappuccino or down a beer until the wee hours. Appetizers and sandwiches make up the menu, but the place is more oriented toward late-night coffee drinking. Musical entertainment is also on tap and ranges from jazz to folk and country.

If your taste buds yearn for the islands, you can get your fix at **Calypso Cafe** (2424 Elliston Pl., 615-321-3878; $$, ☐). This comfortable eatery serves up dishes like tasty rotisserie chicken, greens, coconut-laced muffins, and black beans and rice. Catering is available, too.

Take a seat at the counter or scrunch into one of the well-worn booths of the **Elliston Place Soda Shop** (2111 Elliston Pl., 615-327-1090; $), which holds a special place in the hearts of many Nashvillians. The Soda Shop has been feeding folks for more than 50 years with solid American food. Meat-and-three choices abound here (with great fried chicken and Southern-style veggies), and milkshakes are made the old-fashioned way.

The Gold Rush (2205 Elliston Pl., 615-327-2809; $$ ☐) began dishing out bean rolls before Mexican food became a routine part of American diets. For more than 20 years this rustic dining spot has served the city with both good food and drink. The sometimes-rowdy bar is still a popular nightspot in the evenings.

One of Nashville's institutions is certainly **Jimmy Kelly's** (217 Louise Ave., 615-329-4349; $$–$$$, ☐). This steak house opened in 1934, and has been catering to Nashville's elite ever since. Some waiters have been here 30 years, watching generations of the city grow up. Order a filet and a Faucon salad after downing a platter of the city's best corncakes, and you'll have had a meal in the fine Southern tradition.

Doughnut lovers will want to stop by the too-cool **Krispy Creme** (2103 Elliston Pl., 615-329-1100; $), which looks like a throwback to the '50s with its chrome, brick, and green exterior. If you'd rather grab some on the go, there's a drive-through window. Watch for the "Hot" sign to light up, indicating you can snare a just-from-the-oven doughnut.

Mosko's Muncheonette (2204 Elliston Pl., 615-327-2658; $, ☐) has an array of sandwiches that will satisfy any hunger pangs. Try the Turkey Munch or the Veggie Melt or the addictive Chunky Chicken Salad while you people-watch at the counter. Soups, salads, and homemade desserts round out the experience. The eatery is known for its scrumptious chocolate-zucchini cake and pineapple-spiked hummingbird cake. In the evening drop by for a cappuccino or *caffe latte*. Mosko's delivers and caters, too.

One of the area's newer establishments is **The Owl's Nest Coffeehouse** (205 22nd Ave. N., 615-321-2771; $, ☐). Here's a place to savor espresso (made by a real *barista*—an Italian term for one who knows how to make coffee concoctions) and other java specialties, Italian sodas, *biscotti*, grilled *panini* (sandwiches made with European-style breads, meats, and vegetables), homemade soups, pastries, bagels, and muffins. Live entertainment appears in the evenings, and there are daily newspapers to peruse from around the country. Traditional tea service is offered on Sunday afternoons.

Obie's Pizza (2217 Elliston Pl., 327-4772 $$; □) turned the city onto Chicago-style pizza some 20 years ago and continues to bake the Italian pies. You can't go wrong with the house special—a combination of ground beef, pepperoni, mushrooms, onions, and green peppers.

Red Hot & Blue (2212 Elliston Place; 615-321-0350; $$, □) mixes blues and barbecue, a combination that's hard to beat. Diners can order wet or dry ribs, barbecue brisket, smoked chicken, pork shoulder, salads, and side orders like onion ring loaf and chili. Red Hot & Blue offers casual dining, take-out, catering, a children's menu, and an outdoor patio. The walls are decorated with blues and jazz posters, and occasionally patrons can enjoy live entertainment.

Legions of Vanderbilt students have gotten through school by eating grilled cheeseburgers at **Rotier's Restaurant** (2413 Elliston Pl., 615-327-9892; $). Besides the burgers (which come on buttered toast or French bread), the eatery has homemade mashed potatoes, great salmon croquettes, milkshakes, and heaven-sent lemon icebox pie. The cozy dining spot opened in 1945, and Mrs. Rotier still runs the show from the cash register.

For a taste of England, you can head to **The Sherlock Holmes Pub** (2206 Elliston Pl., 615-327-1047; $–$$, □) for either lunch or dinner. Fish and chips, shepherd's pie, and other British fare is on tap here, and imported beers and Gaelic music on the weekends boost the feeling of the UK.

NIGHTLIFE

Back in the 1970s, the **Exit/In** (2208 Elliston Pl., 615-321-4400) was the place to see people like Joni Mitchell, James Taylor, and Kris Kristofferson. Some of today's hottest groups—R.E.M., Hootie & the Blowfish, and Stan Lassiter—still take the stage here, as do lesser known artists both from Nashville and around the country. The popular late-night spot is known for its roster of alternative, pop, and hard-rock groups that entertain several nights a week.

ACCOMMODATIONS

Many of Nashville's residents were teary-eyed when the old Father Ryan High School came down, but in its place rose a **Hampton Inn** (2300 Elliston Pl., 615-320-6060; $, □) that provides a convenient night's rest for Nashville visitors. The hotel has 157 guest rooms, 33 of which are suites. A free continental breakfast is provided, as well as an outdoor pool.

GREEN HILLS

Green Hills, as the name suggests, is a scenic part of the city surrounded by gently rolling green hills (at least in the spring and summer months). It is a mecca for shoppers, offering a mix of specialty stores and branches of well-known chains. Restaurants also abound in Green Hills, as do offices and tree-lined residential streets. In the middle of all of the commercial activity is Hillsboro High School, a United States School of Excellence with approximately 1,250 students.

ATTRACTIONS

Despite protests about traffic and congestion from some of the residents of Green Hills, **Funscapes,** a $20 million entertainment center is set to open adjacent to The Mall at Green Hills in 1997. Besides housing retail tenants and restaurants, the complex (located at the site of the South Central Bell building) will have a 14-screen theater, "virtual reality" batting cages and golf driving ranges, a 36-hole miniature golf course, an arcade with interactive video games, and a children's maze.

For anyone with a yen for the outdoors, **Radnor Lake** (1160 Otter Creek Rd., 615-377-1281 or 373-3467) beckons with a variety of natural features and planned activities for adults and children (see "Local Treasures" in this section).

SHOPPING

The breadth of stores situated in Green Hills is mind boggling. The area is dense with businesses selling everything from potting soil to lingerie, packed into a commercial district that is not really that large. The following listing covers just a smattering of the stores there.

The most obvious place to shop is **The Mall at Green Hills** (2126 Abbott Martin Rd., 615-298-5478), easily spotted with its green-topped buildings. The center has expanded in recent years, becoming one of the city's tonier places to shop. Dillard's and Castner Knott are the mall's anchor tenants, with neighbors that include Eddie Bauer, Ann Taylor, Casual Corner, The Limited, Nine West, and H2O Plus. Some of these retailers—Brooks Brothers, The Nature Company, Gus Mayer, and Laura Ashley—have their only Nashville location here.

LOCAL TREASURES: RADNOR LAKE STATE NATURAL AREA

In the middle of one of the fasting growing areas of the city lies a quiet sanctuary. Radnor Lake, often referred to as "Nashville's Walden," is a place to see wildlife, hike trails, and commune with nature in all its glory.

Radnor is located in the Oak Hill community, southeast of the downtown area at 1160 Otter Creek Road. Its 1,088 acres surround an 85-acre lake, formed in 1914 when the Louisville and Nashville Railroad Company used it to furnish water for steam engines and livestock at nearby Radnor Railroad Yards. Originally it was also used as a place for L&N officials and their guests to hunt and fish. Then, in 1923, an executive with the railroad company declared the site a wildlife sanctuary at the request of the Tennessee Ornithological Society because birds began using it as a rest stop on their annual migrations.

In the early '70s, the Tennessee Department of Conservation, with help from the federal government and thousands of citizens, purchased the acreage as the first official Tennessee State Natural Area.

Each season at Radnor is distinct and worth a visit. The hundreds of species of wildflowers, ferns, mosses, and other plants dominate in the spring and summer. Fall turns the trees myriad colors, beautifully reflecting off the peaceful lake. And winter, too, is lovely, with bare trees that allow visitors to see more distant vistas. Animals aplenty take shelter here, including geese, herons, coots, frogs, snakes, turtles, lizards, and various mammals.

There are many nature trails, some more difficult than others. The Lake Trail is suitable for children because it's relatively flat. More daring hikers will want to climb the Ganier Ridge Trail for spectacular views of the surrounding area. Or you can stay on the paved road for walking, running, or biking. (Vehicular access is limited to specific residents, drivers with disabilities, and emergency vehicles.) Stop in the Criley Visitor Center for help in choosing a trail.

The Natural Area also offers a wonderful selection of free activities to help familiarize visitors with the site. Night hikes, canoe floats, owl prowls, creek walks, wildflower hikes, and interesting children's programs are scheduled throughout the year. Call (615) 377-1281 or 373-3467 for more information.

With almost 100 stores, this mall is manageable yet provides enough variety for any shopping spree. On Saturdays at 11 a.m. the center becomes a haven for the little ones with "Kid's Club," a fun,

45-minute program of singers, magicians, and other performers who ably entertain audiences of children. Other special programs are scheduled throughout the year, including visits by Santa Claus and the Easter Bunny.

Just off Hillsboro Pike is **Hillsboro Plaza** (3900 Hillsboro Pk.), featuring an L-shaped strip of terrific stores. **Imagination Crossroads** (615-297-0637) specializes in educational toys and also hosts birthday parties for children in the back room. **Chocolate Soup** (615-297-1713) sells children's clothing, offering great prices on brand names. **Levy's** (615-383-2800), a Nashville mainstay since 1874, is also located here, providing both women's and men's clothing for the city's league of conservative dressers. **Uptown's Smoke Shop** (615-292-6866) carries imported cigarettes and cigars, and does custom tobacco blending. This men's haunt also stocks a great selection of coffee beans and smoker's gifts.

Bandywood Drive also boasts an unusual array of retail establishments. **Especially Baby** (2164 Bandywood Dr., 615-298-2323) has beautiful infant clothing and accessories, as well as cribs and other equipment. Also noteworthy is **Tennessee Memories** (2182 Bandywood Dr., 615-298-3253), a place specializing in Tennessee-made products. Both are located in Bandywood Fashion Square.

Bandywood, which almost makes a horseshoe from Abbott Martin Road to Hillsboro Circle, also has a great children's shoe store called **Lonnie Young Shoes** (2203 Bandywood Dr., 615-297-3984), **Lyzon Frames & Fine Art** (2205 Bandywood Dr., 615-385-5198), **Mary-Mary Maternity** (2105 Bandywood Dr., 615-383-5338), **Ward-Potts Jewelers** (2160 Bandywood Dr., 615-298-1404), and **Green Hills Coffee Roaster** (2209 Bandywood Dr., 615-292-2670), just to name a few more nice places to shop.

Botanica (2211 Bandywood Dr., 615-386-3839) is a small neighborhood garden center with knowledgeable owners who can help you find both unusual and familiar plants and flowers to make your garden a showplace. And **The Oriental Shop** (2121 Bandywood Dr., 615-297-0945) can outfit your home with a hand-woven kilim, a Chinese silk, or one of the other fine rugs that are stacked in the store.

It's hard to miss **Grace's Plaza** because of the large clock tower that looms over the shops there. Book lovers will find refuge at **Davis-Kidd Booksellers** (4007 Hillsboro Pk., 615-385-2645), with roughly 100,000 titles covering every subject area, in addition to cards, stationery, gifts, and toys. Book signings are a regular occurrence here, with both local authors as well as national writers stopping by. Upstairs you'll find the terrific Second Story Cafe (see "Dining"), which also draws a crowd for the Friday evening writer's nights. Saturday mornings at 11 finds the upstairs atrium area lively with anxious youngsters who come to see the bookstore's weekly children's show, featuring singers, magicians, and programs based on popular children's authors.

Grace's (4005 Hillsboro Pk., 615-383-8155)—for which the plaza is named—sells upscale designer wear for women and has a very nice shoe salon. Clothes horses will also want to stop at **The Cotton Mill Collection** (4009 Hillsboro Pk., 615-298-2188) for some smart fashions, and at **Private Edition** (4009 Hillsboro Pk., 615-292-8606) for a wide array of cosmetics, perfume, and other personal items geared toward women. The shop also offers facials, massages, and other pampering treatments.

Corzine & Co./Richters Jewelers (4003 Hillsboro Pk., 615-385-0140) is a wonderful place to find a special gift, with china, crystal, and silver in addition to a superb collection of estate jewelry.

Next door is one of the many **Service Merchandise** stores located in our area (3909 Hillsboro Pk., 615-254-2718). This catalog showroom, which got its start in Nashville, carries jewelry, sports equipment, stereos and TVs, toys, and household items.

Turn off Abbott Martin Road to find **Tanner & Company** (2109 Abbott Martin Rd., 615-269-4599), a small specialty store stocking high-design giftware, china, toys, and other goodies. The same strip is home to **Blockbuster Video** (615-269-9555), a place to find all your favorite movies.

Other strip shopping areas include **The Glendale,** with **Pier I Imports** (3730 Hillsboro Pk., 615-269-5059), **Pen & Paper** (2026 Glen Echo Rd., 615-269-0273), **Relax the Back Store** (2020 Glen Echo Rd., 615-460-0004), and **Cook's Nook** (3770 Hillsboro Pk., 615-383-5492), a gourmet cookware store with unusual food items and coffee beans from its sister store—Bean Central on West End Avenue. Just behind The Glendale is **Designer Renaissance** (3706 Hillsboro Pk., 615-297-8822), a consignment store selling brand-name recycled clothes.

In **Green Hills Court,** at 4004 Hillsboro Pike, shoppers will find lingerie at **Rebecka Vaughan** (615-269-4413), art supplies at **The Art Store** (615-298-1112), rare and used books at **Dad's Old Book Store** (615-298-5880), and decorator fabrics at **Calico Corners** (615-269-4551) at the very back of the complex. Next door, gardeners will turn up both supplies and fresh-cut blooms at the **Flower Mart** (4002 Hillsboro Pk., 615-269-5733).

On Crestmoor Road you can find **The Games Store** (2104 Crestmoor Rd., 615-383-4104) and **Bennett Galleries/Frames By U** (615-297-3201) tucked into the same building. The former has a great selection of toys and games (as well as a popular train that circles a track near the ceiling at the back of the store), and Bennett provides unusual frames, artwork, jewelry, household items, and both do-it-yourself or custom-framing services in addition to occasional art exhibits.

Cumberland Gallery (4107 Hillsboro Cr., 297-0296) is a showplace for contemporary art. The white stucco building represents a cadre of both local and national artists, with openings monthly throughout most of the year.

If you're searching for furniture, **Bradford's** (4100 Hillsboro Pk., 297-3541) and **Storehouse** (4108 Hillsboro Pk., 615-385-0812) offer a good selection of furnishings from traditional to contemporary. Bradford's has an Oriental rug department as well.

A few doors down is **Helen's Children's Shop** (4102 Hillsboro Pk., 615-292-3576), where generations of Nashvillians have gone for christening gowns and other fine children's wear.

DINING

When there's a game on, you can count on a mob at **The Box Seat** (2221 Bandywood Dr., 615-383-8018; $, ☐). This cozy den of sports-mania feeds its enthusiasts with burgers, salads, soups, pizzas, and cold beer while they watch teams throw, kick, shoot, or bat the ball.

Bread & Co. (4105 Hillsboro Pk., 615-292-7323; $, ☐) is known for its European-style bread that is baked fresh daily. A loaf of the farm bread or *pane bello* adds to any meal, but you can also sample these delicious baked goods by buying one of the ready-made sandwiches. The menu changes weekly and includes taste treats like portabella mushroom, herb-roasted turkey breast, or jerk chicken. Bread & Co. also sells bagels, scones, and other pastries, and the house blend decaf—one of several flavors of coffee on tap each day—is addictive.

Inside **TIBA** in The Mall at Green Hills is **Chez Nu Nu** (2126 Abbott Martin Rd., 615-269-5121; $–$$, ☐), a sweet retreat from the hustle of shopping. Fresh (and low-fat) salads, soups, and sandwiches popu-late the menu here, along with entrees like vegetable lasagna, *polenta*, and grilled vegetable pizza. Breakfast pastries, homemade *biscotti*, various teas, and cappuccino round out the choices for both lunch and dinner. Eat at the bar (surrounded by cosmetics and beauty aids) or at one of the tables outside the store. TIBA also offers spa treatments, massages, manicures, and makeovers, and even mammograms in conjunction with Columbia/HCA Healthcare Corp.

Tucked inside Hillsboro Plaza is **Chinatown Restaurant** (3900 Hillsboro Pk., 615-269-3275; $–$$, ☐), a popular spot for traditional Chinese fare. Steamed dumplings, crunchy noodles, *lo mein,* and Mongolian lamb are reliable favorites, either inside the nicely deco-rated eatery or on your own dishes at home. Take advantage of the lunch specials, too, which include rice, egg roll, and soup for about $5.

Christie Cookie (4117 Hillsboro Pk., 615-297-0274) is the place to satisfy cravings for fresh-baked cookies. The homegrown company makes an assortment of the hefty treats, including white chocolate macadamia nut, chocolate chip with walnuts, and a fat-free oatmeal raisin. Buy a couple or a whole tin as a gift.

Classic Gourmet (3900 Hillsboro Pk., 615-383-8700; $, □) is known primarily as a gourmet cookstore, but the Green Hills shop also offers tempting salads, soups, and sandwiches, such as tabouleh, orzo and artichoke, black bean, and stuffed pasta shells. The bakery churns out baguettes, croissants, and a variety of sweets, too. Catering is available, and the shop offers great cooking classes with local chefs and other knowledgeable gourmets.

Clayton-Blackmon (4117 Hillsboro Pk., 615-297-7855; $, □) got its start in the catering business and expanded by opening a deli. Now you can either eat there or take home some of the restaurant's favorites, like chicken pot pie (made on Tuesdays), pasta salad, muffuletta, and veggie rollers (vegetables and seasoned creamed cheese rolled up in Armenian flat bread). The menu changes daily, and there are always prepared dinners perfect for warming up at home. Catering is still available as well as Sunday brunch.

Sometimes nothing compares to a hot doughnut. You can find your fill at the **Donut Den** (3900 Hillsboro Pk., 615-385-1021; $), with about 30 varieties of doughnuts, jumbo muffins (including low fat), frozen yogurt, *kolaches* (smoked sausage, cheese, and chives wrapped in bread), and fresh-brewed coffee.

El Palenque (2208 Crestmoor Rd., 615-383-6142; $–$$, □) draws folks in for its authentic Mexican fare, served potholder-hot from the oven. The family-run establishment satisfies with specials like *chili verde*, Mexican beef stew, burritos, enchiladas, and other south-of-the-border favorites for both lunch and dinner. El Palenque has another location on Nolensville Pike.

Although its facade and Art Deco interior have been debated in some circles, the creative entrees and award-winning wine list are what brings locals to **F. Scott's** (2210 Crestmoor Rd., 269-5861; $$–$$$, □). This establishment also serves lunch and Sunday brunch, and live entertainment comes in on Friday and Saturday evenings.

Great Harvest Bread Co. (3900 Hillsboro Pk., 615-298-1032; $, □) is a wonderful place to pick up one of 20 different varieties that this "scratch" bakery makes each day. The onion dill rye, basil Parmesan, and jalapeño corn bread make tasty accompaniments, and the premium white and wheat loaves are terrific for everyday use. Also worth trying are Great Harvest's oatmeal cookies and delicious cinnamon rolls. There are always free samples here to help you decide (or confuse you even more).

The neon squiggle illuminating a white stucco building earmarks the **Green Hills Grille** (2122 Hillsboro Dr., 615-383-6444; $$, ☐), a casual spot for lunch or dinner. The tortilla soup is consistently good, as are the lemon-artichoke chicken, fresh salads, herb-roasted chicken, and "smashed" potatoes. There's even a decent children's menu in this Southwestern-decorated establishment.

Even though it's part of chain, **La Paz Restaurante Cantina** (3808 Cleghorn Ave., 615-383-5200; $$, ☐) knows how to do Southwestern. You can't go wrong here with combinations such as black beans, goat cheese, and fresh spinach in a whole-wheat tortilla, or shredded pork, raisins, almonds, and ancho chile–black bean sauce. This lively eatery serves up fajitas, California quesadillas, margaritas, and a host of beers for both lunch and dinner. During warmer weather, the outdoor deck is a boisterous berth for dining.

If you're in the throes of shopping and want a bite to eat, **Mozzarella's** (2126 Abbott Martin Rd., 615-383-8004; $$, ☐) will take the edge off. Located in The Mall at Green Hills, this dining spot (with tables conveniently located for people-watching) has a well-rounded menu. The goat cheese pizza is a winner, and there's always a fresh catch, pastas, and various tasty sandwiches and salads. Other branches operate on West End Avenue and at Cool Springs.

There's something comforting about eating in a bookstore, and **Second Story Cafe** (top floor of Davis-Kidd Booksellers, 4007 Hillsboro Pk., 385-0043; $$, ☐) is definitely that and more. Maybe it's the homemade soups like tomato basil, or the chicken pot pie, grilled tuna melt, Chinese won ton salad, decadent desserts, and aroma of coffee that put folks at ease. Place your order at the counter, and soon enough a server will deliver the goods. You can fill up in the a.m. with a jumbo muffin or a fresh fruit bowl. Kids will enjoy the PBJ sandwiches or grilled cheese that come on animal-decorated plastic plates for lunch or dinner. Writer's Nights roll out on Friday evenings, also featuring up-and-coming musicians, and Celtic music fills the air on the third Saturday of each month.

With less than a dozen tables, **Shalimar** (4111 Hillsboro Dr., 615-269-8577; $$, ☐) is a homey place to sample the exotic cuisine of India for lunch or dinner. Lamb *biryani, tandoori* chicken, or fish *masala,* with accompaniments like *dal,* rice, and traditional Indian breads, make a fine meal, cooled by a sweet, yogurt-based *lassi.*

If you're craving *tempura, gyoza,* or a California roll, **Shintomi** (2184 Bandywood Dr., 615-386-3022; $$, ☐) can satisfy any yens for Japanese fare. Take in the action at the sushi bar, or dine at one of the many tables in this bright and comfortable Green Hills spot.

Baking bread in addition to a host of decadent concoctions is what draws the famished to **Sweet Art Bakery** (3900 Hillsboro Pk.,

615-385-7265; $, ☐), just a few doors down from Great Harvest. The baguettes and other homemade breads are worth sampling, as are the pastries, cakes, and other sweets. The "chocolate room" allows you to see the confections being made, but if yours isn't a sweet tooth, Sweet Art also serves deli sandwiches at lunch. They cater, too.

In Nashville, comfort food is synonymous with a plate of meat and vegetables. That's what you'll find at **Sylvan Park Restaurant** (2201 Bandywood Dr., 615-292-6449; $, ☐), just one of several branches of this Nashville institution. Fried chicken, meat loaf, country-fried steak, macaroni and cheese, fried okra, turnip greens, and other Southern-style veggies make up the menu. Don't leave without tasting the eatery's chocolate pie—it's legendary.

White Mountain Creamery (4004 Hillsboro Rd., 615-297-0144; $) is one of the few places that makes real ice cream on the premises (check out the two green ice-cream makers in the window, though the churning now takes place in the back). Try raspberry chocolate chip or butter pecan, and forget about fat grams. This Green Hills store also serves frozen yogurt, sandwiches, muffins, and bagels. The other location, on 21st Avenue South, is near Vanderbilt University.

NIGHTLIFE

Tucked into a strip shopping center in Green Hills is the legendary **Bluebird Cafe** (4104 Hillsboro Pk., 615-383-1461; $–$$, ☐), probably the most well-known club in Music City. Owner Amy Kurland has created a cozy nightspot that gives up-and-comers a chance to show what they're made of, which in some cases leads to a record deal and even stardom. There are generally two shows each night, the first of which is free (although there is a nominal food/drink charge per person) and spotlights songwriters and performers trying to break into the music scene. The second show features someone with more name recognition and requires a reserved seat. The nightclub serves soups, salads, sandwiches, and other specials if you want to munch while you listen. Reservations for most performances can be obtained by calling the Bluebird—be aware that most shows sell out quickly!

HILLSBORO VILLAGE/ VANDERBILT

The Hillsboro Village area is dominated by the presence of Vanderbilt University and its 10,000 students. The hub of activity centers around the businesses on 21st Avenue South and nearby side streets. The Village is one of the city's oldest commercial districts—it's dominated the area for more than 75 years, starting in 1920 with two groceries and a pharmacy. In the past few years, the Hillsboro Village Association has improved the street with park benches, bike rails, and trash receptacles, and several new retail stores and restaurants have opened their doors.

Vanderbilt University was named after Cornelius Vanderbilt, who donated $500,000 to the school in 1873, a year after it was chartered by the Methodist Episcopal Church as Central University. This private coeducational institution and its highly regarded medical center give the city much to be proud of. George Peabody College of Vanderbilt University, which merged with Vanderbilt in 1979, is also located on 21st Avenue South. Now a National Historic Landmark, Peabody was established in 1875 to train teachers after the Civil War and became well known for its educational program, remaining so today.

The Peabody Demonstration School, now known as University School of Nashville, sits across the street from the Peabody campus and is one of the city's best private schools. Each winter USN offers a series of adult classes that range from star gazing to songwriting. Most of these inexpensive courses are taught by University School parents and other community members.

ATTRACTIONS

Movie fans who want to see foreign and art films head to the **Belcourt Twin** (2102 Belcourt Ave., 615-383-9140, admission fee). The theater, which was built in 1925, has had a rich history in Nashville. It served as home for the Grand Ole Opry during a couple of years and was the site of the Community Playhouse in 1936. Even when it became a movie house in the '60s, the place was showing the films of Fellini and Truffaut and serving Godiva chocolates. The Belcourt, which has undergone repairs in the past couple of years, is now owned by Carmike Cinemas, who plan to continue to operate it as a foreign and art film venue.

When was the last time you climbed on a sea serpent? You can do just that at **Fannie Mae Dees Park** (Blakemore Blvd. and 24th Ave. S.; free). The colorful mosaic sculpture, which is actually a place to sit, was created by New York artist Pedro Silva and dedicated in 1981. The park has swings, slides, tennis courts, picnic areas, and an almost-too-dangerous tunnel and rock wall that, of course, kids love to scale. This Metro park is one of the few in the city with equipment suitable for use by severely handicapped visitors.

Art classes, exhibitions, movies, and more are found inside the **Sarratt Student Center** on the Vanderbilt University campus (24th Ave. S. and Vanderbilt Pl., 615-322-2471). A variety of instruction in basketry, ceramics, photography, and weaving is offered each semester to students and the general public. The gallery has a year-long schedule of impressive art shows, featuring both students and artists from around the country. Sarratt Cinema shows art and foreign films as well as newly released movies throughout the year, many of which are co-sponsored by the Nashville Film Society. The Sinking Creek Film/Video Festival (615-322-4234) held in November is the oldest film festival in the South and the only one in Tennessee (see "Festivals"). Sarratt also presents a series of dance, classical music, and theater during its "Great Performances at Vanderbilt" series, held in the nearby Langford Auditorium.

SHOPPING

A Thousand Faces (1712 21st Ave. S., 615-298-3304) sells an interesting medley of contemporary gifts, including candles, cards, T-shirts, silver jewelry, scented oils, mirrors, and small pieces of furniture. There's also a shop on Second Avenue downtown.

Years of hoarding books—more than 30,000 of them—induced Sara Lee Woods to open **Bookman** (1724 21st Ave. S., 615-383-6555) and sell her husband's incredible collection of literary works. The inventory contains an assortment of topics, from science fiction to Civil War history, and features rare and used books, most of which are hardcovers.

Bronco Belle (1801 21st Ave. S., 615-292-6447) carries a fine array of Southwestern and Old West–style clothing, leather goods, and other apparel that will make you look like a country music star (even if you can't hum). The store stocks a selection of jewelry, handbags, and belts, too.

For more than 30 years musicians have frequented **Cotten Music Center** (1815 21st Ave. S., 615-383-8947). The tiny shop concentrates on high-end acoustic guitars and all the accompanying equipment.

The Davis family has been involved in Hillsboro Village in some fashion for 25-plus years, owning a hardware store (now run by other owners), **The Needle Craft Shoppe** (one of the oldest of its kind in town, 615-298-4729), and **Davis Cookware & Cutlery Shop** (1717 21st Ave. S., 615-298-4728). The latter was the Village's first coffee shop, opening almost 20 years ago. The store handles coffee beans and equipment (even sells espresso machines for restaurants and services them), gourmet cookware, and a good selection of knives. The business offers knife and scissors sharpening, too.

There are five **Friedman's** stores in the city, but the one near Hillsboro Village is the largest and has been there since the 1970s (2101 21st Ave. S., 615-297-3343). Shoppers can find Army surplus items here in addition to a great selection of jeans, shoes, and camping supplies. Knives, socks, and military emblems are just a sampling of the other stock the store carries.

For cutting-edge contemporary clothing, visit the **Silk Stocking District** (1713 21st Ave. S., 615-383-5640), also run by members of the Davis family. The small boutique sells one-of-a-kind hand-done items, fashions by some of the newer small-scale designers, and tasteful accessories.

Stone Mountain (1602 21st Ave. S., 615-321-5499) takes customers back to the 1960s with black lights, clothing, posters, jewelry, hair color, shoes, toe rings, sunglasses, recycled jeans, dresses, backpacks, and incense. The entranceway, lit with a collection of black-light posters, is a blast from the past.

For fine fabrics and notions, you can't beat **Village Fabrics** (1814 21st Ave. S., 615-383-8896). For more than 35 years this small shop has been serving seamstresses with high-end fabrics and natural fiber materials. Village Fabrics also boasts what is said to be the largest button collection in Nashville, an accumulation gathered from near and far by a lady who has them on consignment at the shop.

DINING

One of Hillsboro Village's newer eateries is **Bongo Java 2** (1812 21st Ave. S., 615-297-8646, $$), a cousin to Bongo Java on Belmont Boulevard (see the "Belmont" section). A great place to stop for coffee (the beans are roasted in-house) and dessert, the cafe also offers ethnic vegetarian fare and other edibles to go, as well as an eclectic group of imported gifts from small coffee-growing communities.

Also new on the street is **Boscos Nashville Brewery Co.** (1805 21st Ave. S., 615-385-0050; $$, ☐). Pizzas, sandwiches, pasta, daily specials, and salads are on tap for lunch and dinner, as are eight varieties of beer brewed on the premises. Boscos, which has another location in Memphis's Germantown, is the only brewer of Steinbier in North America. The age-old process involves using red hot rocks, which gives the beer a caramel flavor.

Brown's Diner (2102 Blair Blvd., 615-269-5509; $) has been a familiar place to drink a beer and munch a cheeseburger since 1927. The satellite dish on the roof is almost as big as the restaurant, which looks more like a small mobile home. Brown's is a dive with character and a hangout for loads of Vanderbilt students.

Tucked inside the Village at Vanderbilt is **Cuisine of India** (1500 21st Ave. S., 615-320-1315; $$; ☐), where you can savor the spices of the subcontinent by dining at the restaurant's huge lunch buffet—serving more than 15 items—or by choosing from the menu of vegetarian favorites at either the noontime or evening meal.

In 1981, **Faison's** (2000 Belcourt Ave., 615-298-2112; $$, ☐) opened in a renovated house and was the first place to offer "creative cuisine." Guests ate on the front porch, front lawn, or inside one of the cozy dining rooms. While the restaurant has undergone some transformations since then (the front porch is now enclosed), the food is basically the same. Broken Hearted Fettuccine can still be found on the menu in addition to a well-rounded selection of other interesting fare. Don't leave without having the "Next Best Thing to Robert Redford," a layered concoction of pecan-shortbread crust, chocolate mousse, cream cheese, and whipped cream. Head to the back of Faison's and you'll step into **Jody's Hot Chicken Club,** a more casual spot for spicy chicken and beer (a totally different atmosphere).

Next door to Faison's is **Iguana** (2000 Belcourt Ave., 615-383-8920; $$, ☐), an eatery (also owned by Jody Faison) that treats diners to New Age south-of-the-border cuisine with choices like brisket tacos and sushi burritos as well as more familiar fare like chicken enchiladas and *chiles rellenos*. A boisterous brood usually gathers at the bar, and it's popular among the younger set.

In the summer months, the softball leagues pile into **Jonathan's Village Cafe** (1803 21st Ave. S., 615-385-9301; $$, ☐). This bustling Hillsboro Village spot serves up tasty "brick oven" pizza combinations (try grilled chicken and herb) in addition to specialty sandwiches, burgers, salads, quesadillas, and an array of appetizers. A covered outdoor area allows diners to check out the people cruising up and down 21st Avenue, and there is live entertainment a couple of times a week.

If you want breakfast, you can't do much better than **Pancake**

Pantry (1796 21st Ave. S., 383-9333; $–$$, ☐), a mainstay in this area since 1961. A new building that went up in 1995 almost doubled the size of the old place (which was next door), but it still serves up hot-cakes, eggs, omelettes, and good joe for that morning kick. It's not unusual to run into some of Nashville's more famous residents at the Pantry, often served by waitresses that have been there since the beginning. Diners can also find bagels, muffins, flavored coffees, and specialty sandwiches on the restaurant's menu.

It's hard to beat the pies from **Pizza Perfect** (1602 21st Ave. S., 615-329-2757; $–$$, ☐). The Hillsboro Village branch offers the same menu as the Granny White Pike location, with pizza (both round and Sicilian), spaghetti, manicotti, and sandwiches served on homemade bread. Besides being good, Pizza Perfect pizzas are *cheap*.

At **Provence** (1705 21st Ave. S., 615-386-0363; $, ☐) you can sample the regional breads of France, baked in ovens much like those used by villagers in that country. A variety of flavors, shapes, and sizes make these great accompaniments to any meal. In addition, there are sandwiches, pastries, and some food products for sale in the cafe.

San Antonio Taco Co. (461 21st Ave. S., 615-327-4322; $, ☐) is the place to "hang" if you're a college student in search of a fast cheap meal. This eatery introduced Nashville to soft tacos, and continues to serve them up stuffed with beans and cheese, chicken, and fajita steak. *Chalupas,* enchiladas, taco salads, and guacamole tacos are also on the menu, as is beer by the bucket. The outdoor deck is a pleasant place to dine if you can get a table.

Sports fans as well as those who don't know an ace from a full-court press are drawn to **Sportsman's Grille** (1601 21st Ave. S., 615-320-1633; $$, ☐) for the lively ambiance and the good food. Burgers (get the grilled onions), salads, sandwiches, and various specials are on tap here, as well as beer and other munchies for watching the game.

When **Sunset Grill** (2001 Belcourt, 615-386-3663; $$–$$$, ☐) debuted in 1990, it was an instant hit as the place to be seen. This nicely decorated dining spot serves both lunch and dinner and is known for dishes like "Beggar's Purse" (phyllo pastry stuffed with crab, shrimp, and mushrooms on bed of sun-dried tomato sauce), Gouda grits with crawfish, and rosemary chicken. Patrons can order a number of heart-healthy entrees, and the outstanding dessert is the chocolate bombe. The outdoor patio with its retractable roof makes for a nice place to sup or watch the stars.

LION'S HEAD/
CHARLOTTE AVENUE

The Lion's Head area, on White Bridge Road, is a convenient shopping spot, especially with the ever-popular Target store located there. The Lion's Head theaters draw lots of people in, as do the many restaurants and stores lining the street. Just past Nashville State Technical Institute is Charlotte Avenue and Interstate 40. Charlotte has a quirky mix of businesses, some of which are worth investigating.

SHOPPING

At the **Beveled Edge** (73 White Bridge Rd., Paddock Place, 615-356-7784), you'll find a terrific selection of frames, posters, limited edition prints, and other home accessories, as well as both custom framing services or do-it-yourself facilities.

You don't have to own a Harley to admire the merchandise at **C & S Harley-Davidson** (4600 Delaware Ave., 615-297-7500), where shoppers can wallow in the whole gamut of motor clothes, T-shirts, riding accessories, and parts for motorcycles. The great-looking chrome-and-glass-block store also boasts the world's largest illuminated bar-and-shield sign.

There's enduring appeal to the sleek lines of Scandinavian-designed furniture, and that's what you'll see lots of at **Scandinavia Center of Design** (73 White Bridge Rd., 615-352-6085). The Paddock Place store also displays a collection of lighting, rugs, woolens, and glassware.

A full line of snow skiing and biking equipment is what the **Ski Mogul** (73 White Bridge Rd., lower level, 615-356-7669) sells. Besides offering repair and rental service, the shop has clothing and accessories for both sports. Another location operates in Hendersonville.

Sprintz Furniture Showroom (325 White Bridge Rd., 615-352-5912) provides an enormous selection of furnishings for the home at 30 to 50 percent off the normal retail price. More than 450 manufacturers are represented in addition to a large collection of fabrics and home accessories. And the in-store designer service makes decorating your home even easier.

Bargain hunters might want to cruise the aisles at **Stein Mart** (92 White Bridge Rd., 615-353-9808) for brand names at a discount. The store brims with clothing for the whole family (as do the other locations at Rivergate and in Brentwood) as well as shoes and accessories, linens, and gifts.

Wilderness Sports Outfitters (73 White Bridge Rd., 615-356-5230) can accommodate the outdoor enthusiast with backpacks, tents, clothing, footwear, kayaks, canoes, and climbing and rappelling equipment. The store even rents kayaks and offers instruction in using them.

DINING

Natural wood and large windows give **Benkay** (40 White Bridge Rd., (615-356-6600; $–$$, □) its pleasant ambiance. Diners can take a seat at the sushi bar, at one of the tables, or for a more intimate meal in one of the restaurant's *tatami* rooms. The *bento* boxes are a great deal (and a lot of food), but you might want to sample some of the other traditional Japanese fare here, too.

There's one restaurant worth visiting that's so far off the beaten bath you really do wonder if you're still in Music City. **Blue Moon Waterfront Cafe** (525 Basswood Ave. at Rock Harbor Marina, 615-352- 5892; $–$$, □) is a fun, floating restaurant on the Cumberland River where the chef puts a creative twist on catfish and trout.

At **Bobbie's Dairy Dip** (5301 Charlotte Ave., 615-385-4661; $), you can still get a tomato stuffed with chicken salad or a corn dog, but the reason to go is for the milkshakes (choices include banana, coffee, and even cantaloupe in the summer) and the chocolate-dipped cones. Order from one of the two windows and grab a spot on the bench or at a picnic table. This throwback to the '50s can't be beat on a hot summer night.

The smell of garlic mixes in the air outside **Caesar's Ristorante Italiano** (88 White Bridge Rd., 615-352-3661; $$, □), making it hard to pass up after a trip to the movies. This cozy dining spot pleases with entrees like homemade meatball subs, shrimp scampi, pizza, stuffed artichokes, *gnocchi,* veal piccata, and Lobster alla Frank Sinatra. Outdoor seating is available, as is a children's menu.

Dalts Grill (38 White Bridge Rd., Lion's Head Village, 615-352-8121; $$, □) bills itself as a classic American grill, and indeed the place looks the part. It's a good spot for burgers, sandwiches, Mexican fare, shakes, and delicious chocolate malt cake. Take a seat at the counter so you can watch the cooks sprint through the orders or dine on the patio.

At **Las Palmas Mexican Restaurante** (5511 Charlotte Pk., 615-352-0313; $–$$, □), you can satisfy south-of-the-border cravings with authentic enchiladas, burritos, and tacos in a no-frills atmosphere. Twenty-five different combinations are offered, so you can have your *chiles rellenos* and *tostada,* too. Several other locations are sprinkled around the city.

The exotic ethnic cuisine of Thailand is what's cooking at **The Orchid** (73 White Bridge Rd., 615-353-9411; $–$$, []). In the nicely decorated surroundings, start with *tom ka kai* soup or *meekrob,* and then taste the *pla lard prig, massaman* curry, *pad Thai,* or Orchid chicken. The coconut crêpes or fried bananas make a sweet finale to a well-prepared meal.

Across the road, yet another region is represented at **Rainbow Key** (80 White Bridge Rd., 615-352-7252; $$, □). This is a popular place for Caribbean cooking, where diners can find smoked fish, coconut shrimp, conch fritters, and Jamaican chicken. Shuck some oysters at the raw bar or head outside to digest some key lime pie. You can also try your hand at laser tag and some of the arcade games at Q-Zar, which is accessible through Rainbow Key a couple nights a week.

MIDTOWN

This area of the city has seen lots of new development in recent years. The epicenter of this commercial district might be the big billboard usually sporting the larger-than-life mug of one of country music's greats. Reba McEntire, Trisha Yearwood, Vince Gill, and the famous duo of Tammy Wynette and George Jones have all graced the signage, which marks the split between West End Avenue and Broadway.

ATTRACTIONS

Step into the **Upper Room Chapel and Museum** (1908 Grand Ave., 615-340-7207; free) for some solitude and to see an interesting collection of religious objects. There is a large wood carving of "The Last Supper" copied from Leonardo da Vinci's painting, artwork from 1330 to 1990, books, manuscripts, English porcelains, furniture, and seasonal displays of nativity scenes and Ukrainian eggs.

Scarritt-Bennett Center (1008 19th Ave. S., 615-340-7500; free) offers spiritual programs, music study, and other multicultural events. The quiet grounds and striking stone buildings are now used for retreats, meetings, and conferences, but this was formerly Scarritt College, known for its leadership in social awareness. The Hartzler-Towner Multi-Cultural Museum in the Laskey Library contains artifacts from all over the world, including costumes, textiles, ceramics, baskets, and wood sculptures. A collection of dolls representing many countries is displayed in 22 cases in the administration building. It's best to call ahead to arrange a time to see the dolls.

SHOPPING

At **Chili Pepper Junction** (909 20th Ave. S., 615-320-5475) you can see if your mouth is made of asbestos or not. Hundreds of hot sauces are stocked here—with names like "Texas Tears," "Dave's Insanity Sauce," and "Capital Punishment"—as well as salsa, seasonings, dry peppers, jam and jellies, and peanuts, all with some sort of burn.

The Great Escape (1925 Broadway, 615-327-0646) sells quite an array of used albums, CDs, cassette tapes, and books, plus a good selection of comic books, movies, postcards, posters, stickers, and books on tape. Two other locations—one on Second Avenue North and Gallatin Pike North—also serve the city.

If it's art you're looking for, you can get your fill at **Local Color Gallery** (1912 Broadway, 615-321-3141). Approximately 100 Tennessee artists are represented here, and their paintings, drawings, photographs, pottery, and jewelry are all for sale.

Lucy's Record Shop (1707 Church St., 615-321-0882) provides a mix of new music and old, stocking CDs, tapes, *and* vinyl. Lucy's is one of the few places that sells new vinyl, and there's also a variety of books, magazines, T-shirts, and accessories geared toward music buyers. Check it out on weekend nights for alternative live music.

Next door to Local Color (same building, different entrance), you can see even more artwork at **Midtown Gallery & Framers** (1912 Broadway, 615-322-9966). Local, national, and international artists' work is on view, ranging from pottery to serigraphs.

Women feel like they're experiencing nirvana when they enter **Off Broadway Shoe Warehouse** (1503 Broadway, 615-254-6242). Literally 30,000 pairs of shoes and boots are housed in the massive store, and all at a discount. The latest styles from running shoes to T-straps fill the racks at Off Broadway, which is only open Thursday through Sunday.

At **Plunge** (1612 Church St., 615-329-0789) you can find alternative apparel for both men and women. The cool dresses, shirts, boots, and more here present a nice change from the mass merchandise you see at the malls. Plus, you can also get your hair cut!

History buffs will want to visit **Southern Historical Showcase** (1907 Division St., 615-321-0639), a store that specializes in the Civil War. Original war-dated documents, historical books, artwork, prints, photographs, maps, autographs, and other collector's items are on hand.

DINING

The Bound'ry (913 20th Ave. S., 615-321-3043; $$–$$$, ☐) might have one of the most interesting interiors in Nashville, with Renaissance-style murals, an attractive horseshoe bar, and penny wall sculpture. The menu is just as intriguing, with a long list of tapas (share across the table) and entrees that epitomize the word *fusion*. Try the wild ravioli, planked trout, or the roasted vegetable bowl. There are daily specials, too, and more than 100 different beers.

Belly up to the large vegetarian buffet at **Country Life** (1917-19 Division St., 615-327-3695/menu line 615-320-1405; $–$$). This Seventh Day Adventist–run establishment brings forth savory choices like eggplant casserole, "sun burgers," spinach fettuccine, homemade soups, and an always-fresh fruit and salad bar. Head outdoors to one of the picnic tables for a meal alfresco.

You can people-watch from the front room of **Danzo's** (212 21st Ave. S., 615-329-0036; $–$$, □), or opt for a cozy booth back in the bar. Here diners can sample Italian fare with entrees like chicken Marsala, veal Parmigiana, shrimp scampi, manicotti, stromboli, and pizza.

DaVinci's Gourmet Pizza (1812 Hayes St., 615-329-8098; $$–$$$) was the city's first gourmet pizza place, serving up pies chock full of ingredients like feta cheese, scallops, capers, pineapple, and red cabbage. The "Southwestern," an amalgamation of spiced chicken, pinto beans, mozzarella cheese, onions, green pepper, and cilantro, is a taste treat. Fresh pesto can be substituted for tomato sauce, and soy cheddar is available for those who want a nondairy pizza. DaVinci's delivers and also has outdoor seating.

If you're craving tasty, good-for-you fare, head to **Garden Allegro** (1805 Church St., 615-327-3834; $, □). Burritos, salads, beans, curries, pastas, and daily specials like grilled rainbow trout and black bean chili will make a satisfied vegetarian out of the most die-hard meat eater.

You can experience culinary showmanship at your hibachi table grill or enjoy the quiet seclusion of the sushi bar at **Goten** (110 21st Ave. S., 615-321-4537; $–$$, □). The Stone Grill is an impressive entree (with meat and vegetables served on a sizzling rock), and the sushi is always fresh. The *tempura* and rice bowls also give diners a tasty glimpse of Japan.

Granite Falls (2000 Broadway, 615-327-9250; $$, □) has established itself as a place to consume imaginative food in pleasant surroundings. The all-weather patio is perfect for people-watching, and you can't beat the black bean soup and rotisserie chicken.

If you want to sample some of the flavorful food of the islands, **Jamaica** (1901 Broadway, 615-321-5191; $$, □) will satisfy those cravings. Raw oysters, jerk chicken, crab cakes, and side dishes like Daddy Dee's beans and peas, mango salad, and cheese biscuits attract diners, as do the live music and salt-water aquariums.

Time hasn't changed much about **Mack's Cafe** (2009 Broadway, 615-327-0700; $, □). Since 1920 this small, modest eatery has been serving typical country cooking, with dishes like pot roast, barbecue, mashed potatoes, turnip greens, cream-style corn, black-eyed peas, and squash casserole. Mack's burgers are also a often-ordered item from either the long counter or the well-worn booths.

For more than 30 years, **Mario's Ristorante** (2005 Broadway, 615-327-3232; $$–$$$, □) has been attracting patrons for its Northern Italian cuisine. This award-winning restaurant treats guests to delicious entrees in a warm and inviting atmosphere. A selection of fine wines accompany dishes like *ossobucco, salmone al vino bianco,* and *pollo arrosto.* Don't leave without trying the *pasta ai tre colori,* a sampling of three pastas that changes with the season.

Painted in a soft palette of colors and featuring changing art exhibits, the cozy **Midtown Cafe** (102 19th Ave. S., 615-320-7176; $$–$$$, ☐) pleases with a well-prepared Caesar salad, lemon-artichoke soup, and entrees featuring fresh fish, pastas, lamb chops, and veal.

The Mill Bakery Eatery & Brewery (1918 Broadway, 615-327-3500; $–$$, ☐) boasts home cooking with a flair, serving up dishes like wild mushroom and peppercorn meatloaf, basil chicken fettuccine, Colorado calzone, white pizza, and the Mill Melt. The in-house bakery churns out bread, bagels, and muffins, and a variety of hand-crafted beer is brewed on the premises.

The Nashville Country Club (1811 Broadway, 615-321-0066; $–$$, ☐) isn't a private association at all. Rather, this bustling eatery is a place where Music-Rowers, Midtown workers, and other diners feast on wood-fired pizzas, sandwiches, salads, smoked or grilled dishes, and a buffet-style breakfast on Saturdays. You can even be a part of the "club" by purchasing some of the NCC clothing that's for sale.

Slice of Life Bakery & Restaurant (1811 Division St., 615-329-2525; $–$$, ☐) started serving health food before enlightened eating was hip, and it continues to offer well-made soups, sandwiches, entrees, and macrobiotic selections. Tiger Food, a mix of sautéed veggies, scrambled tofu, brown rice, nutritional yeast, diced tomatoes, green peppers, and light cheese, will really give you something to roar about, and the daily special is always a winner (not strictly vegetarian, either). Wash down whatever you eat with the iced herbal tea. Live music on weekday evenings and for Sunday brunch makes this airy spot a nice place to dine, or stop by for some wholesome cookies, muffins, cakes, and other baked goods to go.

"Southern urban cuisine" is what's on tap at **South Street Original Smokehouse, Crab Shack and Authentic Dive Bar** (907 20th Ave. S., 615-320-5555; $–$$, ☐). Here they rustle up smoked meats, barbecue shrimp, Memphis-style ribs, po'boys, and a lot of other creative fare. The outdoor tables are popular in the warmer months, and occasionally you see crawfish boils conducted in the middle of the dining room.

One of the city's newest dining spots is **Trilogy** (1911 Broadway, 615-321-8818; $$–$$$, ☐), which specializes in Mediterranean food with a California spin. Innovative salads, pastas, fresh fish, and beef entrees can be enjoyed in an interior personally designed by country star Naomi Judd, whose husband is a partner in the business. Restaurant rooms are named for daughters Wynonna and Ashley, thus making the "trilogy."

Synchronized dining and fine food with a French flair sets **The Wild Boar** (2014 Broadway, 615-329-1313; $$–$$$, ☐) apart from the other restaurants in town. That and its 15,000-bottle wine inventory. The Wild Boar is the only Tennessee restaurant to win *Wine Spectator*'s Grand Award. Try lunch here if your pocketbook is limited— you'll get to sample the wonderful fare at a reduced price.

MUSIC ROW

Music Row, situated primarily on 16th and 17th avenues, is a collection of record companies, trade organizations, publishing companies, publicity firms, recording studios, attractions, and shops. It's a world onto itself and a great place to get a sense of the immense popularity of country music.

For fans, the strip of stores on Demonbreun Street is heaven on earth. Where else can you see a reproduction of Barbara Mandrell's bedroom, Elvis Presley's gold Eldorado, and one of Hank Williams's guitars? Plus souvenirs abound of country music's best-loved stars, from Conway Twitty to Ernest Tubb.

Trolley service runs through the Music Row area if you would rather hitch a ride. Call Nashville Trolley Co./MTA at (615) 862-5950 for schedules and fares. On summer weekends, riders are sometimes entertained by trolley singers.

ATTRACTIONS

At the **Car Collectors Hall of Fame** (1534 Demonbreun St., 615-255-6804; admission fee), visitors can see Webb Pierce's silver-dollar 1962 Bonneville, a 1982 Buick Riviera built for Tammy Wynette, Louise Mandrell's MG, Roy Acuff's last touring car, and Marty Robbins's black 1934 Packard, as well as the Batmobile from the *Batman* television series. There are also period fashions from the early 1900s, musical instruments, and a Nifty Fifties Gift Shop.

The **Country Music Hall of Fame and Museum** (4 Music Sq. E., 615-256-1639; admission fee) is a place to get a close-up view of the world of country music and the legacy it leaves behind. Visitors can see 3,000 items related to country music and exhibits devoted to the Grand Ole Opry, country music and the movies, and songs and songwriters. Plus, there are vintage film clips, memorabilia from old and new country music stars (including Elvis Presley's "solid gold" Cadillac), and a terrific gift shop with souvenirs that aren't easily found anywhere else. Don't miss Thomas Hart Benton's mural titled "The Sources of Country Music" in the museum. The Country Music Hall of Fame is just an extension of the Country Music Foundation, the world's largest and most active research and exhibition center dedicated to this form of music.

Admission to the CMHF includes a tour of RCA Studio B, the city's oldest remaining studio where Elvis Presley, Chet Atkins, Dolly Parton, and lots of other stars recorded their hits. Recent renovations made the studio a working facility for recording again and brought it back to the way it looked in the 1960s. Visitors can now watch a recording session there as well as take a guided tour. A free trolley ride (with museum admission) will transport you to Studio B and provide a bit of history about the Row along the way (museum-goers can also ride any trolley free during the rest of the day).

While you can occasionally see a country star in Music City, you're probably better off visiting the **Country Music Wax Museum and Mall** (118 16th Ave. S., 615-256-2490; admission fee). Here 60 life-size wax country stars are on view (some looking more realistic than others), dressed in clothes owned by the entertainers. In addition, you can see stage costumes and instruments and browse the mall shops, which offer everything from T-shirts to records and Christmas items.

The **George Jones Museum** (27 Music Cr. E., 615-255-9119; free) is primarily a gift shop, but there's also a mini-museum with some of Jones's gold and platinum records, photographs, and stage outfits.

The **LeGarde Twins Country Music Theatre** (1407 Division St. in the Music Row Quality Inn, 615-822-3322; admission fee) puts on live country music shows with both up-and-coming entertainers and traditional favorites. Both day and evening shows are offered, so call ahead for the schedule.

Barbara Mandrell Country (1510 Division St., 615-242-7800; admission fee) is probably the largest complex on Music Row. Fans of the blond singer can see a reproduction of her bedroom, personal items like clothes and guitars, a video tour of her log home, and a huge gift and Christmas shop.

At **Recording Studios of America** (1510 Division St. underneath Barbara Mandrell Country, 615-254-1282; admission fee), you can record your own song just like the stars. The studio provides the background music, and you sing your best soprano or bass. You end up with a cassette to play for your friends.

The **Hank Williams Museum and Gift Shop** (1524 Demonbreun St., 615-242-8313; admission fee) looks like just a place for souvenirs, but the museum is in the back. The memorabilia here pertains to both father and son ("Are you ready for some football?"), with a look at their successful country music careers. See stage outfits, guitars, and photographs, and watch a video that details the lives of both Sr. and Jr.

MUSIC VALLEY/AIRPORT

Even though the whole Opryland complex seems to be a world unto itself, there are other surrounding businesses and restaurants that draw people to this area northeast of downtown. Music Valley Drive is home to many country music–themed attractions and is right across the street from the Opryland Hotel. And clustered near the Nashville International Airport are numerous hotels to accommodate overnight travelers.

ATTRACTIONS

Cruise the Cumberland River on Opryland USA's *General Jackson* (2802 Opryland Dr., 615-889-6611; admission fee), said to be the world's largest showboat. Morning, midday, evening, and specialty cruises run year-round on this 300-foot paddle wheeler. Food and entertainment, ranging from live bands to Broadway-style shows, make the boat a popular attraction. Midnight cruises churn the river during Fan Fair in June, and special holiday rides entertain passengers in November and December. The boat is available for parties and receptions, too.

One of the newest attractions in the area is **Gold River Mining Co.** (2416 Music Valley Dr., 615-391-8994; admission fee), where you can prospect for precious and semiprecious gems and then take them home. Or you might want to let one of the on-site jewelers make a pendant or earrings from your find. In a separate area you can pan for natural gold, too.

If you're looking for some fun outside the walls of Opryland, head to **Grand Old Golf** (2444 Music Valley Dr., 615-871-4701; admission fee). Three miniature golf courses, bumper boats, and a video arcade will entertain the kids for hours.

There is a cluster of three museums (2802 Opryland Dr., 615-871-6611; free except for parking) that appropriately encircle the Grand Ole Opry House in the **Opry Plaza** area as you enter the entertainment resort. (By the way, the Opry House hosts a variety of performances other than the Grand Ole Opry. Concerts by big-name artists and even that purple dinosaur we all love also take to the stage here).

At the **Grand Ole Opry Museum,** visitors can learn about the history of the Opry, the world's longest running radio show. Special

LOCAL TREASURES: GRAND OLE OPRY

Since its beginning in 1925, the Grand Ole Opry has showcased the top entertainers in the country music genre, giving airtime to both newcomers and veterans alike. Every Friday and Saturday evening (and during matinees in the summer), the live radio broadcast on WSM-AM 650 has come across the airwaves to millions of listeners and to the 4,400 people inside the Grand Ole Opry House here in Music City. And the Opry hasn't missed a broadcast since it began, making it the longest running radio show in the world.

The Opry started as "The WSM Barn Dance" and followed an NBC network radio show called "The Music Appreciation Hour." One night in 1928, announcer George D. Hay said, "For the past hour, we have been listening to music taken largely from Grand Opera, but now we will present 'The Grand Ole Opry.'" That was the beginning of a tradition that continues today.

The popularity of the show grew, and after moving to several locations in the city, the Opry landed at the Ryman Auditorium in 1943. There, for some 31 years, stars would take to the stage to entertain the many fans of country music.

Up until 1938 the program was mainly instrumental, until a young Roy Acuff stepped up to perform with his Smoky Mountain Boys. Others vocalists followed, like Ernest Tubb, Hank Williams, Bill Anderson, Grandpa Jones, Kitty Wells, and Johnny Cash. Today more than 70 performers are part of the Grand Ole Opry cast. And what's remarkable still is that each show is unrehearsed, so you never know who might stop by for some picking and singing.

The schedule of 20 to 25 acts isn't usually finalized until about 48 hours before the program begins, and there is no advance promotion. (Summer matinee performances showcase 8 to 10 artists.)

Present-day performers stand on an eight-foot circle of hardwood taken from the Ryman stage and placed in the Opry House. George Hay summed up the Opry phenomenon by saying, "The Grand Ole Opry is as simple as sunshine. It has a universal appeal because it is built upon good will, and with folk music (it) expresses the heartbeat of a large percentage of Americans who labor for a living."

Tickets for Opry performances, which range from $12.50 for matinees to $16.50, can be reserved by calling (615) 889-6611, or by writing Tickets, 2808 Opryland Drive, Nashville, TN 37214.

electronic displays, interactive video devices, and a variety of sets tell the stories of legendary stars like Patsy Cline, George Jones, Marty Robbins, and Hank Snow. Even present-day Opry stars are represented, and there are replicas of recording studios, the Ford pickup from a couple of Clint Black videos, stock cars raced by Robbins, and a six-part video on the history of the Opry narrated by Porter Wagoner.

A great collection of vintage musical instruments rewards visitors in **Roy Acuff's Musical Collection Museum.** More than 200 stringed instruments, family heirlooms, and memorabilia about the "King of Country Music" are placed on display in this structure.

Next door, at the **Minnie Pearl Museum,** the "Queen of Country Comedy" is honored with exhibits that chronicle her life and her comedy. A photo gallery includes memorable career moments and many poses with friends.

When people say they're going to the lake, they usually mean **J. Percy Priest Lake** (3737 Bell Rd., 615-889-1975; free). The variety of outdoor recreation opportunities creates the draw, including sailing, fishing, canoeing, skiing, hunting, camping, picnicking, and hiking. The lake, which is run by the U.S. Army Corps of Engineers, is approximately 42 miles long, and it's impounded by the J. Percy Priest Dam near Interstate 40 that serves for hydropower and flood control. There are a few commercial marinas nearby that provide access to the river and boat rental. The visitors center is located at the resource manager's office, immediately upstream from the dam on Bell Road.

If you're interested in cars of the stars, check out **Music Valley Car Museum** (2611 McGavock Pk., 615-885-7400; admission fee). Here visitors can see antique vehicles like a 1914 Model T and cars owned by country music greats George Jones, Dolly Parton, Chet Atkins, and Randy Travis, as well as Elvis Presley. Also located here is Shotgun Red's Collections, a group of the famous "dummy's" knives, player piano, Harley-Davidson motorcycle, Shotmobile, airplane, and gifts from fans. Shotgun Red, who gained attention on the *Nashville Now* television show, can still be seen on day cruises aboard Opryland USA's *General Jackson* showboat.

Country music fans can take in more than 50 life-like wax figures of country artists at **Music Valley Wax Museum of the Stars** (2515 McGavock Pk., 615-883-3612; admission fee). There are also costumes and a "Sidewalk of the Stars" with 250 autographed hand- and footprints.

A 1794 plantation home houses the **Jim Reeves Museum** (1023 Joyce Ln., off Gallatin Rd., 615-226-2065 or 226-2062; admission fee). Follow Reeves's career in country music and admire a wide range of personal items, including furniture, guitars, stage costumes, gold records, and a 1960 Cadillac Eldorado he drove.

For fans of long-time country music makers Kitty Wells and Johnny Wright, you won't want to miss **Kitty Wells/Johnny Wright Family Country Junction** (240 Old Hickory Blvd., about 5 minutes from Opryland, 615-865-9118; free). There's a replica of Kitty's kitchen, old photos, a 1957 Cadillac used in *Coal Miner's Daughter,* and lots of gifts, including a Kitty Wells cookbook.

It's not often that you can combine breakfast and entertainment, but fortunately it's the case at **Nashville's Breakfast Theater** (2620 Music Valley Dr., 615-329-2091; admission fee). Guests can get their fill of both an all-you-can-eat buffet and a variety show featuring Grand Ole Opry stars Del Reeves, Jeannie Seely, and other guest artists.

Kids and adults of all ages will enjoy the **Nashville Toy Museum** (2613 McGavock Pk., 615-883-8870; admission fee). There are vintage trains (running through seven-foot mountains), 150-year-old china dolls, early European bears, model ships, doll houses, and a slew of toy soldiers in action. The collection has been featured in magazines and on television and is nationally known for its range of antique toys.

Like the rest of the **Opryland USA** complex (2802 Opryland Dr., 615-889-6611; admission fee), the theme park expanded in 1995 with two new rides: "The Hangman," an inverted roller coaster, and the "Skycoaster," which gives thrill-seekers a ride comparable to hang gliding. Opryland is known as "the home of American music," with entertainment suitable for the whole family. The popular park boasts more than 120 acres of rides, 12 live musical shows, 45 shops, numerous games, a variety of restaurants, a petting zoo, and a "soft play" area with slides and mazes for the little ones.

Opryland USA River Taxis (2802 Opryland Dr., or Riverfront Park, 615-889-6611; admission fee) transport riders from the Opryland complex to downtown or vice versa on 57-foot boats that carry 100 passengers. Even though there have been complaints about the wear and tear the boats bring to the banks of the Cumberland River, the 45-minute ride is offered daily, year-round. Call for schedules or stop by the Opryland Ticket and Information booth (or the Wildhorse Saloon or Ryman Auditorium if you're downtown).

TNN: The Nashville Network (2806 Opryland Dr., 615-883-7000) is a cable television station that beams into more than 64 million homes in the United States and Canada. Visitors can see shows in production and be a part of the studio audience at the facilities at Opryland or at the Wildhorse Saloon downtown. Many of the shows require reservations beforehand, so it's best to call ahead. TNN

Viewer Services (615-883-7000) can tell you about production schedules and the talent lineup.

Besides finding a large assortment of gifts, the **Willie Nelson and Friends Showcase Museum** (2613A McGavock Pk., 615-885-1515; admission fee) has memorabilia from Nelson as well as big names such as Ernest Tubb, Elvis Presley, Porter Wagoner, and Patsy Cline.

SHOPPING

All of your shopping needs are easily met at **Factory Stores of America** (545 Outlet Center Dr., 615-885-5140). This complex of more than 65 shops features everything from clothing to china. Well-known businesses like Cape Isle Knitters, Duck Head, Reading China, Carter's Childrenswear, Bugle Boy, Rack Room Shoes, and Black & Decker are just some of the retail attractions situated across from the Opryland Hotel.

DINING

Claiming to have the "world's best catfish," **Cock of the Walk** (2624 Music Valley Dr., 615-889-1930; $$, ☐) serves up the barbeled catch—deep-fried of course—as well as chicken and shrimp. You'll spot license plates from near and far in the attractive gray building's parking lot, drawing folks in for the family atmosphere and reasonable prices.

At the **Nashville Palace** (2400 Music Valley Dr., 615-885-1540; $$, ☐), you can dine on catfish and prime rib, hear live entertainment nightly, and even dance. It's a popular spot, serving tourists and residents alike for almost two decades. And it's where country star Randy Travis launched his career.

NIGHTLIFE

When the clock strikes 12 on Saturday nights, the **Ernest Tubb Record Shop Midnight Jamboree** (2414 Music Valley Dr., 615-889-2474; free) starts its live radio show with music by Grand Ole Opry stars (many of whom come over after their live Opry performances) as well as by up-and-comers. The Texas Troubadour Theatre is the site for the show, which started in 1947 and is broadcast every Saturday night on WSM-AM 650. Otherwise, you can stop by the shop for records, CDs, and tapes by all your favorite artists.

Nashville On Stage (2808 Opryland Dr., 615-889-6611) is a series of concerts held in the Chevrolet/Geo Celebrity Theater in the Opryland theme park from March through October. Stars like Lorrie Morgan, Willie Nelson, Patty Loveless, Aaron Tippin, and the Statler Brothers entertain visitors with evening performances (and some afternoons) in the 4,000-seat theater.

Veteran entertainers Boots Randolph and Danny Davis & The Nashville Brass take to the stage most evenings at the **Stardust Theatre** (2416 Music Valley Dr., 615-889-2992 or 800-828-2764). The two-hour variety show features jazz, pop, country, and big band tunes in a 600-seat theater. Call for the current schedule because oftentimes the musicians are out on the road entertaining.

A wide variety of entertainment takes place in the **Texas Troubadour Theatre** (2416 Music Valley Dr., 615-885-0028), including the Ernest Tubb Record Shop Midnight Jamboree, the Nashville Country Showcase, and the Bluegrass Jamboree. The nearly 500-seat venue also attracts crowds on Sunday mornings for the Nashville Cowboy Church, a free interdenominational service where country artists perform their favorite gospel tunes.

ACCOMMODATIONS

Numerous hotels near the airport and Opryland span all price ranges, and several campgrounds are located near the massive complex, too.

The **Nashville Airport Marriott** (600 Marriott Dr., 615-889-9300; $$, ☐) with 18 floors and approximately 400 rooms is convenient if you come in and have to fly out the next day. Accommodations here include indoor/outdoor pools, a health club, an in-house restaurant and lounge, and free coffee and newspapers.

Opryland Hotel (2800 Opryland Dr., 615-889-1000; $$$, ☐) will become the seventh largest convention/resort hotel in the country with the addition of The Delta, bringing the number of guest rooms to almost 3,000. Numerous ballrooms, meeting areas, and an exhibition hall enhance the guest facilities, and the hotel is a popular spot for many local events. Seven restaurants operate in this massive hotel, the newest being Beauregard's, a 400-seat eatery located in The Delta. The latter, said to be the largest construction project in Nashville's history, is a 4½-acre "interiorscape" of 15 stories that includes a flowing river, 25-passenger flatboats, shops, an 85-foot fountain, an indoor garden with 110-foot-wide waterfall, and an elevated walkway, all under one of the largest glass roofs in the world. The hotel added the Springhouse Golf Club in 1990, an 18-hole course designed by well-known golfer Larry Nelson.

The Conservatory, a two-acre garden under one of the largest glass roofs in the world, is also part of the hotel. There are paths through the greenery, benches on which to rest, places to eat and drink, and guest rooms in between. More than 10,000 plants representing 215 species are enclosed here, where the facilities are modeled after conservatories in England, Scotland, Italy, and Canada. A 72-foot fountain sculpture, the Crystal Gazebo, highlights the area.

Christmas is celebrated in a big way at the Opryland Hotel, with musical stage shows, international Christmas dinners, and an arts, crafts, and antique show (see "Festivals"). There is always something on tap at here, so it's worth a visit even if you plan to sleep in your own bed.

The **Sheraton Music City Hotel** (777 McGavock Pk., 615-885-2200; $–$$, □) is conveniently located near the airport and five miles from Opryland. Some 400 rooms and more than 50 suites await guests, along with indoor/outdoor pools, a fitness facility, tennis courts, outdoor jogging trails, a video checkout, and 24-hour room service. The hotel has a restaurant and two lounges and provides shuttle service to the airport, Opryland, and downtown Nashville.

NORTH NASHVILLE/
GERMANTOWN

North Nashville is an area steeped in history and one with its own hidden surprises. Three of the prominent universities in the city are located here, plus it's home to Hadley Park, established in 1912 and thought to be the first public park for African Americans in this country. Today the park contains baseball fields, tennis courts, picnic shelters, and a playground area, and offers a venue for popular summer concerts. The city's African American community was also the first in the nation to have a black-owned-and-operated savings institution, the One Cent Savings Bank, which started in 1904 and is now known as Citizen's Bank.

A section of North Nashville was dubbed "Germantown" for the many German immigrants who settled in the neighborhood during the late 1850s. The area was included in the first map of Nashville, drawn by land surveyor David McGavock in 1786, and was part of the original 960 acres granted to McGavock's brother, James. Germantown is listed in the National Register of Historic Places and was revitalized in the 1970s. Architecture varies from Italianate townhouses to workers' cottages, and original wrought-iron fences and brick sidewalks can still be seen along the streets. The community comes alive each October for a merry Oktoberfest celebration (see "Festivals").

ATTRACTIONS

The 19-acre **Bicentennial Mall** (600 James Robertson Pkwy., 615-532-0001) was built to celebrate the state's 200th birthday in 1996 and is now a Tennessee State Park. The outdoor history museum extends from the state capitol to Jefferson Street and was modeled on the mall in Washington, D.C. Visitors here can see the Path of Volunteers—inscribed granite bricks from families who donated money to the project—as well as a 250-foot state map (also in granite) and the Walk of Counties, with historical information about each. The Walk of History marks major events in Tennessee's history, and a memorial to World War II veterans is also planned for the site. The nation's largest carillon, with 95 chimes (for each Tennessee county), will peal here eventually, but for now don't miss the Rivers of Tennessee, with 31 fountains symbolizing the state's major river systems. The area will serve both as a green space (with a terrific view of the attractive capitol building) and as a place for concerts and other programs within its 2,000-seat amphitheater.

Fisk University (1000 17th Ave. N., 615-329-8500), known in its early days as the Fisk School, started in 1866 as a free school for Nashville's black population. Jubilee Hall, a National Historic Landmark, was the first permanent structure built for the higher education of African Americans in the United States. Money for the building was raised by the Jubilee Singers, who went on worldwide singing tours that brought them international acclaim (and in turn saved the university from financial collapse). A portrait of the original group done by Queen Victoria's court painter hangs inside Jubilee Hall. The Aaron Douglas Gallery in the university library contains a large collection of African art, including masks, musical instruments, ceremonial objects, and more than 200 drawings by Cyrus Baldridge. And the Carl Van Vechten Gallery, located in the school's old gymnasium, houses an important collection of art donated by Georgia O'Keeffe (see "Local Treasures" in this section).

Also in the area is **Meharry Medical College** (1005 D. B. Todd Blvd., 615-327-6111), originally the medical department of Central Tennessee College. Started in 1876 as the first medical education program for African Americans in the nation, the school is now the country's largest private institution for training black health-care professionals. Meharry has educated more African American doctors than any other medical college in the world.

One of the most unusual collections in Nashville is housed in the **Museum of Tobacco Art and History** (800 Harrison St., 615-271-2349; free), tracing the history of tobacco and its role in our country since it was first raised in Jamestown, Virginia, in 1612. The exhibits also tell the story of the crop's economic and social development in other countries. The museum opened in 1982 and currently operates inside the modern United States Tobacco Manufacturing Co. building. Pipes from all over the world, European snuff boxes, Chinese snuff bottles, peace pipes, wood carvings, tobacco jars, and tobacco signage are on permanent display, plus there are rotating exhibits throughout the year from both public and private collections as well as a gift shop with an interesting array of items.

Artifacts from all parts of Africa will soon be on display at the **Sanokofa-African Heritage Museum** (Winston-Derek Center/ MetroCenter, French Broad and Dominion, 615-321-0535). Sculptural carvings, costumes, and a variety of tribal items—some dating back to 1441—will educate visitors, plus occasional music and dance performances as well as lectures and other special programs will also be scheduled here.

LOCAL TREASURES: CARL VAN VECHTEN GALLERY

A very uncommon art collection is found at Fisk University's Carl Van Vechten Gallery, located at the corner of Jackson Street and D. B. Todd Boulevard. Famous American painter Georgia O'Keeffe presented 101 works of art to the university in 1946 with a dual purpose: to ensure that people who may not get a chance to visit the galleries and museums of New York City could see fine examples of modern art, and to provide a collection to an institution that might have difficulty acquiring such treasure.

The Alfred Stieglitz Art Collection, housed in the university's old gymnasium, was part of the famed photographer's collection. This grouping, which is only a portion of the works Stieglitz accumulated, was first shown in 1949, after the gym was renovated. But because of the need for restoration and preservation, the collection was in storage for some 10 years before it was reintroduced to the city in 1984 in a modernized gallery.

The works on view include some of Stieglitz's photographs of O'Keeffe, who late in life became his wife, as well as paintings by O'Keeffe, Charles Demuth, Paul Cézanne, Arthur Dove, George Grosz, Marsden Hartley, John Marin, Pablo Picasso, Diego Rivera, Florine Stettheimer, Auguste Renoir, and Henri de Toulouse-Lautrec.

Several African sculpture pieces are also in the collection. Stieglitz was said to be the first in this country to exhibit works of art by African natives at a showing in 1914.

The Carl Van Vechten Gallery, named for the well-known photographer and chairman of the Fine Arts Department at Fisk in 1949, also hosts a variety of rotating art exhibitions, with many focusing on contributions by African American artists of note.

The gallery is open Tuesday through Friday and Saturday and Sunday afternoons, and there is a suggested contribution. For more information, call (615) 329-8720.

Tennessee State University (3500 John A. Merritt Blvd., 615-963-5000) began in 1912 as the Tennessee Agricultural and Industrial State Normal School. It became TSU in 1969 and is known for its African studies program and women's track coach Edward Temple, who has produced more Olympic medal winners (including the late Wilma Rudolph, for whom a women's residence facility was named in 1995) than any other university coach.

SHOPPING

Summer isn't complete without a trip to the **Farmers Market** (900 Eighth Ave. N., 615-880-2001), which was built in 1995 to replace the old market and accommodate the state's Bicentennial Mall. Approximately 300 vendors hawk farm-fresh produce, garden plants, herbs, and crafts in the market's open-air sheds. Inside the building, shoppers can find The Mad Platter Deli (a branch of the Germantown restaurant), Swett's Farmers Market (see "Dining" in this section), specialty and ethnic stores, a fresh seafood market, a meat market, and other vendors. Gourmet candy, Indian and Jamaican foods, and JB's Hot Stuff (with an endless array of spicy victuals) are just a few of the goodies that attract customers to the $6 million structure, easily recognized by the ears of corn that decorate the exterior.

In the Gallery (624-A Jefferson St., 615-255-0750) provides a place to admire (and purchase) art by a cadre of local artists as well as authentic tribal work from Africa. Rotating exhibits throughout the year fill the gallery's front room, and an assortment of works by artists the gallery represents (including proprietor Carlton Wilkinson's striking black-and-white photographs) awaits browsers in the back room and upstairs.

Collectors can find baseball cards, T-shirts, pennants, books, jackets, posters, and other memorabilia at the **Old Negro League Sports Shop** (1213 Jefferson St., 615-321-3186), which pays tribute to the teams of days gone by.

DINING

Soul food doesn't get much better than what you can find at the **C & J Diner** (405 31st Ave. N., 615-329-1120; $). Try the beef tips, fried chicken, or meat loaf alongside greens, okra, beans, potatoes, and other well-tended side dishes, and don't forget the cornbread. C & J gets awful busy at lunchtime, and often the person in front of you will order the last pork chop, so arrive early. This modest eatery feeds early risers, too.

Unusual food in a unique neighborhood is the cachet of Germantown's **The Mad Platter** (1239 Sixth Ave. N., 615-242-2563; $$–$$$, ☐). An innovative menu tempts diners here, with entrees that draw influences from California and French cuisines. Pasta Mad Platter—a fusion of fresh spinach, artichoke hearts, sun-dried tomatoes, chorizo sausage, mushrooms, onions, fresh herbs, and linguine—is a popular selection, as is the rack of lamb moutarde. Dinner can either be a *prix fixe* five-course meal or a medley of à la carte dishes.

Lunch, served weekdays, is much more casual. Catering is also available, and The Mad Platter has a deli in the Farmers Market that offers sandwiches, prepared foods, and other gourmet goodies.

Some of the best barbecue around gets dished up at **Mary's Old Fashion Bar-B-Que** (1108 Jefferson St. 615-256-7696; $). There are no tables here, just two windows to take orders for ribs, shoulder, chicken (which comes "bones and all" on white bread), and pork sandwiches, best washed down with a bottle of strawberry soda. Side orders of beans, coleslaw, potato salad, and corncakes add to the fixings. Mary's is open 24 hours a day, every day of the year, and has been for more than 30 years.

For Southern food served family-style, try **Monell's** (1235 Sixth Ave. N., 615-248-4747; $$, □). Pass around the bowls of vegetables that come with your entrees here, but don't pass up the homemade desserts or the country breakfast offerings available on Saturdays. Just like home, you can also grab some coffee, and then rock on the front porch and read the paper at this turn-of-the-century Germantown establishment.

More soul food is on tap at **Swett's Restaurant** (2725 Clifton Ave., 615-329-4418; $, □), a part of Nashville's dining scene since 1954. Plate lunch meats like fried chicken, country-fried steak, and ribs are great with greens, sweet potatoes, and vegetable casseroles on the side. The family-run eatery also has a take-out area if you're on the run.

SOUTH NASHVILLE

This area of the city, southeast of downtown, is worth a visit for the plethora of ethnic eateries stretching out along Nolensville Road. The thoroughfare is also a haven for bargain hunters, with several salvage stores and other discount-type businesses. The strip extends all the way from downtown to the road's namesake of Nolensville, Tennessee.

The Berry Hill area has seen much new growth. In addition, a $15 million renovation has attractively updated 100 Oaks Mall, which was the largest shopping center in Tennessee when it opened in 1967. Media Play, TJ Maxx, CompUSA, Totally 4 Kids, PetsMart, and Off Fifth (the Saks Fifth Avenue outlet) are located here, as well as several other outlet stores. A Home Depot superstore will take up residence across the street from 100 Oaks, and nearby Bransford Avenue continues to attract interesting small businesses that range from a futon store to a craft gallery.

ATTRACTIONS

Grassmere Wildlife Park (3777 Nolensville Rd., 615-833-1534; admission fee) fell on hard times early in 1995, and its future looked grim. However, the Friends of Grassmere, a volunteer group of people dedicated to the park, reopened the zoological/education center with the help of the city, and the small-scale preserve still features animals that are indigenous to Tennessee. Cougars, black bears, elk, bison, river otters, wolves, and other wildlife make their homes here in natural habitats. In addition, the Croft Center has an aviary with native birds, a bee hive, and fish, reptiles, and other aquatic species in the Cumberland River exhibit. The three-quarter-mile trail takes you past each animal and provides a nice (but not too tiring) outing for children. There is an interesting gift shop inside the visitors center for purchasing nature-themed items, and a snack bar also operates. Future plans call for restoration of the historic 1810 Croft House and developing heritage seed gardens and a period farm near the home.

SHOPPING

Besides being able to have your own artwork framed at **The Frame Place and Gallery** (3931 Nolensville Rd., 615-331-1140), you can find paintings, drawings, and crafts for sale here. The Frame Place also stages art openings and shows for some of the national and local artists it represents. Its sister store is Midtown Gallery & Framers.

Music lovers will have a heyday at **Phonoluxe Records** (2609 Nolensville Rd., 615-259-3500). Here you can prowl among rows of used compact discs, tapes, and records, including many out-of-print items. Phonoluxe will also buy your used CDs, tapes, and records, even those dating back to the 1950s.

Shubha Enterprises (2516 Nolensville Rd., 615-242-0204) stocks all of the interesting foods you need for preparing an authentic Indian meal. Staples like basmati rice, lentils, and fresh produce can be purchased here, in addition to spices, Indian teas, and *chapati*. This small Indian grocery also carries frozen dinners to take home, such as lamb *samosas,* chicken curry, and cooked vegetables. Shubha does catering, too.

DINING

Since 1948 **Bar-B-Cutie** (5221 Nolensville Rd., 615-834-6556, $–$$, □) has been serving Nashvillians plenty of pork shoulder, baby back ribs, and mesquite-grilled chicken. Southern-style side orders round out the meals. And if you'd rather dine at home, there's a drive-through window, too.

The **Boardwalk Cafe** (4114 Nolensville Rd., 615-832-5104, $$, □) is the place to go for food and music. The restaurant/club entertains with a varied schedule of bands seven nights a week, offering both writer's and blues nights plus well-known musical groups. A full menu is on tap for both lunch and dinner, featuring salads, prime rib, crab legs, and sandwiches.

The lively flavors of the Caribbean entice at the **Calypso Cafe** (722 Thompson Ln., 615-297-6530; $$, □). This is the third and newest location of the eatery, which specializes in dishes like jerk chicken, black beans and rice, and coconut-laced muffins.

The most prevalent ethnic group by far on Nolensville Road is Mexican, and it doesn't get much better than **La Hacienda Tortilleria** (2615 Nolensville Rd., 615-833-3716; $). An open grill allows diners to watch the cooks make the fresh and tasty *tortas,* tacos, and burritos. Chicken, pork, and beef dishes (tongue and brain, too) come with a sliver of avocado, fresh cilantro, and a wedge of lime. Wash it all down with some *aguas frescas,* sweetened water flavored with tamarind or other fresh fruits. A wide array of Mexican groceries can be found adjacent to the modest dining area, including the freshly made tortillas that are prepared in a building behind the restaurant.

El Palenque (4407 Nolensville Rd., 832-9978; $–$$, □) has been packing folks in since this small eatery since opened in 1983. Sizzling hot plates of Mexican specialties like *carnitas* (braised pork nuggets), enchiladas, fajitas, and *chiles rellenos* are accompanied by refried beans and Spanish rice. The combination dinners are a bargain and let you try more than one entree. There are also vegetarian specials and a child's menu. Another location operates in Green Hills.

New Asia Chinese Restaurant (3744 Nolensville Rd., 615-315-0066; $–$$, □) entices eaters with its huge buffet, featuring several steam tables full of well-prepared appetizers, main dishes, and desserts. Unique to New Asia is its Mongolian Bar-B-Que, which is a confusing term to most Tennesseans. Diners choose a plate of noodles, vegetables, meat, and one of five sauces, and then a cook sautés it all together on a "Mongolian grill." There's also a complete menu to order from, too.

For a taste of Thailand, head to the **Siam Cafe** (316 McCall, 615-834-3181; $–$$, □). Here you can sample dishes that fuse exotic flavors like lemon grass, coconut, ginger, curry, garlic, and cilantro. The *tom ka kai* soup is soothing and spicy at the same time, and the *pla lard prig* (a whole deep-fried snapper topped with a sweet/spicy sauce) and *pad Thai* (Thailand's national dish combining chicken, noodles, bean sprouts, peanuts, and egg) are worth sampling. Siam offers steam tables with a variety of dishes, but opt for a table and order off the menu for a true taste of this foreign land.

WEST END AVENUE

West End Avenue is a major artery through Nashville, and the homes that line the street just west of Interstate 440 are some of the city's most distinctive. The historic Richland–West End district has its share of attractive residences, too, making this a choice area for families and those interested in refurbishing older homes.

The street becomes much more commercial on its way toward downtown. Part of Vanderbilt University lies along West End, including the school's Fine Arts Gallery—housed in the old gym—where visitors can see a wide variety of changing art exhibitions. Students frequent many of the area's restaurants and shops.

ATTRACTIONS

One of Nashville's most popular spots is **Centennial Park** (West End Avenue and 25th Ave. N.; free), which is home to the Parthenon (see "Local Treasures" in this section). The flat green space opened to the public in 1903, six years after the Centennial Exposition honoring 100 years of Tennessee statehood. City leaders who wanted to preserve the Parthenon replica and the Centennial grounds as a public park helped initiate the city park movement in Nashville. The 132-acre common area was originally a farm, but had stints as the state fairgrounds and as a racetrack known as West Side Park.

The park holds quite a few monuments and memorials, some of which date back to the Centennial Exposition. The Civil War Powder-Grinding Wheels, used by Confederate soldiers to grind gunpowder and now displayed in the northeast corner of the park, were exhibited at the 100-year celebration.

The Centennial Art Center—site of the former swimming pool—houses art classes as well as exhibitions. In addition, the park has another building that serves as an activities center for a variety of programs and classes. Kids enjoy climbing aboard the steam locomotive, gazing up at a fighter plane, and seeing the ducks in Lake Watauga. The Sunken Gardens offer a nice spot for a stroll, and many times you can witness a wedding taking place there. The band shell hosts both musical and theatrical performances, including a series during the summer by the Nashville Symphony. The wide expanse of lawn in front of the Parthenon plays host to several arts and crafts festivals during the year, and visitors will find a playground and picnic tables here, too.

LOCAL TREASURES: THE PARTHENON

Nashville's moniker as the "Athens of the South" was first used in an 1840 speech, when the young city was referred to as the "Athens of the West" by the president of the University of Nashville. Philip Lindsley compared Nashville to the Greek center of democracy and scholarship because of the city's active political climate and its commitment to education. "West" soon changed to "South" as the boundaries of the country stretched out to the Pacific coast.

Later, however, the nickname became even more appropriate when the first full-scale replica of the Parthenon was built for the 1897 Centennial Exposition. It was meant to be a temporary structure, constructed of brick, wooden lathe, and plaster. But because it was so popular, the city left it standing. Centennial Park opened around the structure in 1903. However, by 1920 the Parthenon needed a facelift, so the Park Board decided to reconstruct the famous building in concrete. The interior was redesigned with the idea to replicate the floor plan of the original Parthenon in Athens, Greece.

The new edifice opened in 1931 and attracted 10,000 visitors from 46 states and 12 foreign countries in its first month. The striking structure remained virtually unchanged until 1987, when a new east-end entrance, gift shop, and visitor facilities were added. The lower level galleries and offices were also updated in the two-year, $2 million project. In 1994 another multimillion-dollar restoration project began to fix some of the exterior problems, and that process is ongoing.

There is a lot to admire outside about the building itself, which is the only full-scale replica in the world. Its massive Doric columns, bronze doors (thought to be the largest matching set of bronze doors in existence, weighing 7½ tons each), and pediment sculptures that show scenes from Athena's life at either end of the exterior give the building its arresting presence.

Inside, visitors can see Athena Parthenos, a 42-foot sculpture done over eight years by local artist Alan LeQuire. She is the tallest piece of indoor sculpture in the Western world and stands on a five-foot-high marble pedestal. Athena's outstretched palm holds Nike, the winged goddess of victory, and her left hand and arm support a 36-foot spear and a 17-foot shield.

The lower galleries are the site for rotating art exhibitions and house the Cowan Collection of American Art, 63 paintings that have been part of the Parthenon since its second opening in 1931.

The artwork was received by the City of Nashville between 1927 and 1929 as an anonymous gift. Only after James M. Cowan died in 1930 was his name revealed as the donor of the 19th- and 20th-century American paintings.

Casts of the original Elgin Marbles, housed in the British Museum in London, line the sides of the main hallway and depict figures used in the exterior pediments. The Elgin Marbles are actual sculptural fragments of the original Parthenon pediments that were scattered after an explosion in 1687.

The working models that were used to create the larger figures in the pediment sculptures are situated beyond Athena, on either side of the Treasury, which takes its name from the room where all the treasures for Athena were kept. Four Ionic columns are found here.

The site has a nice gift shop, with clothing, games, jewelry, original art, and reproductions of Greek antiquities. The Parthenon is open Tuesday through Saturday, with extended hours during the summer. There is an admission fee, and group rates are available. For information, call (615) 862-8431.

Probably the biggest draw at the **Centennial Sportsplex** (222 25th Ave. N., 615-862-8480; admission fee) is the ice skating rink, especially since it's the only one in town. Kids and adults can take to the ice year-round at the facility, run by Metro Parks and Recreation. There's also an Olympic-sized swimming pool, a large tennis complex, a sports shop, and a whole roster of classes for the exercise enthusiast.

Elmington Park (West End and Bowling avenues, adjacent to West End Middle School; free) is much smaller than Centennial Park, but it still attracts families for the manageable playground and grassy area. The 13 acres, originally part of Edwin Warner's estate, sport tennis courts, too, in addition to being a good spot for special events and occasional cricket games.

SHOPPING

A. J. Martin Jewelers (2817 West End Ave., 615-321-4600) isn't easily categorized. The owner stocks just a few of everything, from chandeliers to artist-made sterling silver jewelry. There is a good selection of fine estate jewelry, too, alongside recycled ornaments, toys, household collectibles, and other unusual giftware.

One whiff is all it takes to reel coffee lovers into **Bean Central** (2817 West End Ave., 615-321-8530) for a cup of java and some freshly roasted beans to take home. The shop stocks all kinds of flavors—both caffeine-laced and decaf—and coffee accessories and serves sandwiches and desserts in a cozy, computer-outfitted room.

If you're looking for new wheels, head to **The Bike Pedlar** (2910 West End Ave., 615-329-2453). More than 200 bicycles are packed into the showroom, and the longtime Nashville store also offers expert repair service. A slew of necessary biking equipment is for sale here, too.

Bittner's (2825 West End Ave., 615-329-3456) leads a double life. The outward image is that of a staid tuxedo store, where those on their way to fancy do's can rent or buy formal wear. During the month of October, however, Bittner's bulges with costumes, masks, and other Halloween accessories guaranteed to scare the neighbors. The store rents costumes during the rest of the year, too, but Halloween is when the place hops.

Walk in one side of **Cumberland Transit** (2807 West End Ave., 615-321-4069 or 327-4093) and you'll see bicycles. Cross over to the other side, and there's a camping store. The former sells mountain and racing bikes, as well as baby joggers, tandems, and equipment. Cumberland offers in-line skating and bike rental, and does custom frame fitting and repairs. Tents, backpacks, canoes, climbing gear, fly-fishing provisions, clothing, shoes, and camping products are stocked across the hall, and the employees are quite knowledgeable about the great outdoors.

If you're searching for hip clothes, stop at **Dangerous Threads** (2404 West End Ave., 615-320-5890), where many entertainers have their garments designed. This is a place for those looking to make a statement. Another location operates on Second Avenue North.

Besides offering pampering services like European body treatments, aromatherapy sessions, and massages, **Essential Therapy** (2817 West End Ave., 615-321-2639) stocks a terrific array of natural body lotions, bath salts, essential oils, and other personal hygiene products.

At **Fleming's** (2922B West End Ave., 615-327-1252) you can find fabulous handmade boots, custom-made Western hats, sterling silver belt buckles, vests, belts, bolos, and even leather bowls. Oftentimes the rustic store stages trunk shows, where you can meet with the craftspeople that customize the items sold here.

The French Shoppe (2817 West End Ave., 615-327-8132) carries designer wear at a discount and is a good place to find "cotton cashmere" clothing as well as accessories like socks, belts, jewelry, and handbags.

Futons Unfolding (2809 West End Ave., 615-329-2444) has been outfitting Nashvillians with futons since 1986. Beds, chairs, tables, lamps, pillows, toys, picture frames, rugs, candlesticks, clocks, and more are stocked at this pleasant store. Also check out the outlet store (2814 12th Ave. S., 615-292-0330), called **Futons on Paris,** where you can find closeouts and scratch-and-dent items.

One finds an unlikely yet successful combination of offerings at the **Greater Vision Gallery** (2817 West End Ave., 615-321-4887). Here visitors can see changing art exhibitions by local/national artists and also have their nails done (in the back room).

For the hippest selection of glasses in town, head to **Image Optical** (2404 West End Ave., 615-327-1614), where you're sure to find specs that will not only make a statement but help you focus on the world around you. Full eye examinations are available here as well.

It's easy to spend time wandering through **Made in France** (3001 West End Ave., 615-329-9300), where you'll encounter all kinds of wonderful things for the home. The store imports both antique and new furniture from France and has a great assortment of ironwork, art, accessories, and gifts.

At **The Produce Place** (4000 Murphy Rd., 615-383-2664) you can rest assured you'll get the freshest vegetables and fruit as well as friendly service. There's a good selection of natural foods, coffees, breads, and dairy products, too, in the Sylvan Park neighborhood shop.

Folk art and comfy South American imported apparel is what shoppers can expect at **Scarlett Begonia** (2805 West End Ave., 615-329-1272). Known for its fabulous selection of sweaters, the store also boasts a good collection of jewelry, belts, hats, tapestries, and other handmade gifts.

Stone Mountain (2308 West End Ave., 615-320-0782) sells posters, incense, clothing, shoes, and other merchandise that reflects the days of love, peace, and flower children. The black-light-lit stairway will take you instantly back to the '60s.

Tower Records (2400 West End Ave., 615-327-3722) offers one of the best selections of tunes in every genre. Folk, jazz, country, alternative, and mainstream pop music lines the shelves, and Tower also stages special events with local musicians.

Imported clothing from South America, Indonesia, and India is what **Wild Animals** (2813 West End Ave., 615-321-0255) specializes in. Shoppers enjoy browsing through brightly colored dresses, belts, shirts, pants, T-shirts, earrings, headbands, backpacks, jewelry, and folk art from around the world.

DINING

At **Amerigo** (1920 West End Ave., 615-320-1740; $$, ☐) you can nibble on tasty pizzas, twirl sauce-laced pasta onto your fork, or savor heartier offerings like shrimp scampi, veal lasagna, or chicken Parmesan. This Italian/American eatery bustles at both lunch and dinner.

The distinctive fare of Korea is well prepared at **Arirang** (1719 West End Ave., 615-327-3010; $$, ☐). Here diners can experience open-flame cookery and prepare their own dishes at the grill/table. Big bowls of wheat noodles or rice topped with veggies and meat, *bulgogi* (gingered beef), and a variety of side dishes like spiced tofu, pickled garlic, and black beans provide a nice alternative to American cuisine.

Blackstone Restaurant & Brewery (1918 West End Ave., 615-327-9969; $$, ☐) turns out some great specialty beers that complement the restaurant's brick-oven pizzas, soups, sandwiches, and entrees like black bean chicken, yellowfin tuna, and baby back ribs. The large bar draws beer enthusiasts in to simply taste what's on tap.

Just a short distance off West End Avenue in the Sylvan Park neighborhood is **Bro's Cajun Cuisine** (4501 Murphy Rd., 615-385-0052; $$), a real dive of a place. But the red beans and rice, jambalaya, *boudin*, and daily lunch specials are as authentic as the grub you get from Cajun Louisiana, owing to the fact that the owner hails from there.

For years the **Cakewalk Restaurant** (3001 West End Ave., 615-320-7778; $$–$$$, ☐) has been one of the leaders in creative contemporary cuisine. Chicken Charleston (grilled chicken with wild mushroom demi-glace, garlic mashed potatoes, and fresh asparagus) is a winner, as is the Tour de France (white beans, tomatoes, spinach, and penne pasta with herbs in white wine). The turquoise-colored walls serve as an avenue of display for local artists, and the dining spot offers daily specials, a terrific brunch, and a chocolate framboise dessert to die for.

The **Cooker Bar & Grille** (2609 West End Ave., 615-327-2925; $$, ☐) attracts crowds for its heaping portions of pot roast, lasagna, macaroni and cheese, sweet potatoes, and other regional fare. The vegetable plate is hard to beat at this family-friendly place, and the salads are also fresh and hefty. Three other locations operate throughout the city.

You can find sandwiches, salads, soups, and desserts at **Ham 'N Goodys** (2829 West End Ave., 615-329-0193; $–$$, ☐). This is a popular spot for ordering spiral-sliced hams and honey-roasted turkeys or picking up party trays and lunch boxes, too.

Some days there's nothing better than biting into a pulled chicken sandwich with white barbecue sauce, and that's what **Hog Heaven** (115 27th Ave. N., 615-329-1234; $–$$; ☐) features. That and beef brisket, pork, spareribs, turkey breast, white beans, potato salad, black-eyed peas, and several flavors of Zapp's potato chips. Catering, too, is available, or buy what you like by the pound.

It's a chain all right, but **Houston's** (3000 West End Ave., 615-269-3481; $$, □) can't be beat for its inviting atmosphere and its consistent salads, soups, burgers, ribs, and toasted cheese bread. The windows allow for people-watching, and the bar area is a hot spot for the younger set.

Kobe Steaks Japanese Restaurant (210 25th Ave. N., 615-327-9081; $$–$$$, □) is the place to see chefs work their magic at the hibachi grill, twirling, chopping, seasoning, serving, and mesmerizing tablemates. After the performance, diners can dig into plates decorated with tender steak, chicken, or shrimp and crisp vegetables.

Sports types like to visit **McCabe Pub** (4410 Murphy Rd., 615-269-9406; $$, □) for a brewski while they catch a game on one of the eatery's many TVs. But McCabe also cranks out some good burgers, vegetable casseroles, and homemade desserts to suit anybody's hunger pangs.

There are a lot of new bagel shops on the block, but the granddaddy of catering to cravings for these chewy delights was Nashville Bagel Co., now called **New York Bagel** (3009 West End Ave., 615-329-9599; $). Fresh bagels, cream cheese, deli sandwiches, soups, baked items, and a coffee bar make the spot popular any time of day. (You can also buy the bagels at area grocery stores.)

The Plaza Grill at Loews Vanderbilt Plaza Hotel (2100 West End Ave., 615-320-1700, ext. 1440; $$–$$$, □) is a pleasant place to dine, with specialties ranging from grilled lamb chops and Atlantic salmon to free-range chicken, plus sandwiches like turkey-apple and grilled chicken club. This hotel restaurant offers a breakfast buffet in addition to regular menu items.

Mexican for the masses takes on new meaning at **Rio Bravo Cantina** (3015 West End Ave., 615-329-1745; $$, □), which serves hordes of Vanderbilt students. Enter the fray by munching on nachos, burritos, and fajitas (and sipping a margarita) inside this West End Avenue eatery or dine outdoors on the patio. Rio Bravo is open for lunch, dinner, and Sunday brunch.

The name pretty much tells you what to expect at **Ruth's Chris Steak House** (2100 West End Ave., 615-320-0163; $$$, □). Located in the bottom of the Loews Vanderbilt Plaza Hotel, this place is known for its prime beef, but guests also can enjoy lobster, salmon, steaks, seafood, chicken, veal chops, pork loin, and lamb chops. All menu items come à la carte.

At **Scholtzsky's Deli** (2404 West End Ave., 615-320-9777; $, □) you can savor sandwiches on fresh-baked buns, salads, and individual-sized sourdough crust pizzas. Try the hot pastrami and swiss on rye, or opt for a bacon, tomato, and mushroom pizza. Another location operates on Second Avenue downtown.

The essence of India comes through the kitchen of **Sitar** (116 21st Ave. N., 615-321-8889; $$, ☐). The vegetarian entrees here are superb, especially with the mint and mango chutneys served alongside. Sitar also serves lamb, chicken, and seafood specialties, *biryanis, tandoori,* and dishes cooked in an Indian iron skillet. The lunch buffet allows you to sample a good variety of this aromatic food.

The small white house known as the **Sylvan Park Restaurant** (4502 Murphy Rd., 615-292-9275; $) has been serving meat-and-three platters to diners for almost 40 years. Fried chicken, turnip greens, corn, baked ham, pork chops, and macaroni and cheese represent just a few of the offerings. Don't dare leave without a piece of chocolate pie (order it with your meal to ensure a slice). Three other locations are situated around the city.

Tin Angel (3201 West End Ave., 615-298-3444; $$, ☐) beckons diners with healthy entrees, spotlighting fish, grains, fresh vegetables, and inventive sauces and salsas. Veggie croquettes, Cajun pasta, chicken *schnitzel,* the hot smoked turkey sandwich, and interesting specials of the day make this a popular lunch and dinner stop.

Time has stood still at **Vandyland** (2916 West End Ave., 615-327-3868; $). The comfy booths, counter, and old-fashioned milkshakes will make you forget what year it is. The sliced chicken sandwich followed by a chocolate drift is sure hard to pass up. Others swear by the double-decker club and a milkshake. Plus you can buy turtles, Rice Krispy treats, and other confections at the front counter.

ACCOMMODATIONS

At the **Hampton Inn** (1919 West End Ave., 615-329-1144; $, ☐), guests can enjoy easy access to Midtown and Downtown. Approximately 170 rooms, including 120 non-smoking accommodations, are available. A free continental breakfast is provided, and other amenities include an exercise room, outdoor pool, and free local calls and cable television.

You couldn't get much closer to Dudley Field than the **Holiday Inn Vanderbilt** (2613 West End Ave., 615-327-4707, $–$$, ☐). Because of its prime location, the hotel fills up fast for university events. Lodgers will find 300 rooms, a coffee shop, the Commodore Lounge (featuring live local music), an outdoor pool, and a fitness center, plus this Holiday Inn property serves a complimentary breakfast.

The **Marriott Courtyard** (1901 West End Ave., 615-327-9900; $–$$, ☐), one of Nashville's newest hotels, has 134 guest rooms, two suites, an exercise room, and a full-service restaurant serving breakfast and lunch. Guests can also dine next door at Valentino's and charge the meal to their room.

Not only is the **Loews Vanderbilt Plaza** (2100 West End Ave., 615-320-1700 or 800-235-6397; $$–$$$, □) a lovely place to spend the night, but it's a hot spot for many local social functions. The hotel, conveniently located near Vanderbilt, offers 338 rooms, 12 suites, two concierge floors and a business-class floor, in-room fax machines, an exercise room, gift shops, the Plaza Grill, Ruth's Chris Steakhouse (see "Dining"), a business center, and tons of meeting space.

ON THE OUTSKIRTS

Nashville has a number of places to go within 30 minutes that are certainly worth the drive. For more information on these and other sites, you might want to refer to *Day Trips From Nashville* (Two Lane Press, 1994), which notes some 24 trips within a two-hour drive of the city.

FRANKLIN

Browsers love the eclectic shops on Franklin's **Main Street,** which vary from one of the largest quilt stores in the country to a place selling Silver Queen corn and tomatoes. The 15-block downtown area is listed on the National Register of Historic Places and provides a step back in time when compared with bustling Nashville. Walking tours can familiarize you with the notable buildings.

Several restaurants in the historic district offer a pleasant chance to dine, or you can take in a movie at the restored 1936 **Franklin Cinema** while munching on pizza or Buffalo wings.

And history buffs won't want to miss **The Carter House** or **Historic Carnton Plantation and Confederate Cemetery,** both significant sites during the Civil War.

Attractive bed-and-breakfast facilities operate in and around Franklin if you want to spend a night or so away from the city life, and four annual festivals provide a good excuse to visit this historic town, located south of Nashville.

For more information, contact the **Williamson County Chamber of Commerce** (615-794-1225), or stop by the **Heritage Foundation Visitor Center** at 209 E. Main Street (615-790-0378).

HENDERSONVILLE

You'll want to drive (or take a tour) northeast to Hendersonville to see the **residences of country music stars** who live here. Porter Wagoner, Johnny and June Carter Cash, Kitty Wells, Lorrie Morgan, and Hank Snow all have homes in Hendersonville, and there are a couple of museums worth a stop if you're a fan of the music. The **Bell Cove Club** has built a reputation on music and food, and many times local greats like Bill Monroe or Ricky Skaggs drop by with guitar in hand. Volleyball, horseshoes, a boat dock, and miniature golf also make this a fun place to visit. And **Historic Rock Castle,** a limestone home furnished in the late 18th-century style with many of owner General Daniel Smith's original pieces, is open to visitors. For more information, call the **Hendersonville Area Chamber of Commerce** (615-824-2818).

HERMITAGE

East from Nashville is the community of Hermitage, Tennessee, known for **The Hermitage,** the home of President Andrew Jackson after his years in the White House. The restored mansion, gardens, and museum give visitors a glimpse of Jackson's life both in Tennessee and Washington. The Greek Revival–style home, situated on 625 acres, still holds many of Jackson's original furnishings. Old Hermitage Church, Tulip Grove (a home built for relatives of the family), several outbuildings, and a graveyard are also on the grounds. There is a well-stocked gift shop with books, crystal, antique jewelry, and Tennessee food products, as well as Rachel's Garden Cafe, where you can grab a bite to eat. Call (615) 889-2941 for more information.

JOELTON

Heading northwest from Music City, you will reach the small community of Joelton. The **Nashville Zoo** and its 600 animals provide a great day of adventure for the family. Tigers, zebras, monkeys, birds, and giraffes make their home here, and there is a reptile house and children's petting area, too. The zoo schedules a wide variety of events during the year, and memberships are available.

Also of note in the Joelton area is **Shadowbrook,** a Tudor mansion that offers dining by appointment in a family home. An elegant meal, accompanied by china, crystal, flowers, and family heirlooms, awaits visitors to the 1929 residence, which sits on Lake Marrowbone. You can find out more about the Joelton area by calling the **Cheatham County Chamber of Commerce** (615-792-6722).

RIVERGATE/ANTIOCH

Both of the Rivergate and Antioch sections of Nashville have a large concentration of shops and restaurants. The Rivergate area, up I-65 north, is dominated by **Rivergate Mall,** with four large anchor stores and about 160 other shops and restaurants. **Hickory Hollow Mall** in Antioch, which is east of the city, is the mainstay of this busy neighborhood, with many of the businesses located off of Bell Road. Like the Rivergate area, Antioch is a hub for discount stores, chain restaurants, and other specialty shops.

FESTIVALS

JANUARY

Nashville Boat and Sport Show. A variety of boats and marine recreation products are on view during this show at the Nashville Convention Center. Fishing seminars, vacation ideas, and entertainment are scheduled throughout the five-day event. (314) 567-0020.

FEBRUARY

Annual Americana Spring Sampler Craft, Folk Art, and Antique Fair. More than 200 country craft and folk art professionals and antique dealers from 30 states gather at the Tennessee State Fairgrounds for this four-day event. Lectures, exhibitions, demonstrations, and entertainment round out the festivities. (615) 227-2080.

Antiques and Garden Show of Nashville. This annual benefit for Cheekwood spotlights horticultural and garden designs, antiques, and decorative arts. Nationally recognized speakers lecture, and there is a tea room on the show floor at the Nashville Convention Center. (615) 352-1282.

Bobby Jones Gospel Explosion. Music and inspiration come together over several evenings as Bobby Jones and a host of other musicians entertain audiences. There are also symposiums, TV tapings, autograph sessions, fashion shows, and inspirational speakers. (615) 665-1009.

Faux Gras. Mardi Gras Nashville-style is what Faux Gras is all about. It's a three-day celebration complete with music, costume balls, a Faux Gras king and queen, and dancing in the streets of downtown. (615) 255-4727.

Heart of Country Antique Show. This annual smorgasbord of antiques features more than 150 dealers from across the country at the Opryland Hotel. All types of furniture, folk art, textiles, and other Americana are showcased, and there are lectures and seminars open to the public. (314) 862-1091 or (800) 862-1090.

MARCH

Nashville Lawn and Garden Show. Gardening displays, horticultural products and equipment, free lectures, and information on making your yard a showplace draw people to this spring event at the Tennessee State Fairgrounds. (615) 352-3863.

APRIL

Designers' Show House. Each year the Junior League of Nashville transforms someone's home into a showcase of the latest in interior design. In addition there's a lecture series, a tea room and gift shop, and a live auction of antiques. Visitors can also partake in a "Dine by Design" series of dinners by area restaurants. (615) 269-9393.

Gospel Music Week. Five days of seminars and concerts culminate with the annual Dove Awards, which honor the best in gospel music. The events take place at The Renaissance Nashville Hotel downtown. (615) 242-0303.

Southern Women's Show. The Nashville Convention Center is the gathering place for women who want to attend an event geared exclusively toward them. More than 400 exhibits and demonstrations present everything from fitness to food. Fashion shows, a celebrity kitchen, and other seminars are also scheduled. (704) 376-6594/tickets (800) 849-0248.

Tin Pan South. Sponsored by the Nashville Songwriters Association, this annual music festival celebrates the wordsmiths behind the tunes. A golf tournament kicks off the event, and a Legendary Songwriters Acoustic Concert is the finale at the Ryman Auditorium. During the week, some of the country's top performing songwriters appear at local clubs. (615) 251-3472.

MAY

Historic Rural Life Festival. Each May the Oscar L. Farris Agricultural Museum fascinates folks with a weeklong schedule of activities like sheep sheering, butter churning, craft demonstrations, and wagon rides. Kids can also see and touch farm animals. (615) 360-0197.

Iroquois Steeplechase. The second Saturday in May brings hordes of folks to Percy Warner Park to see one of the best known steeplechase events in this country. The Iroquois, which benefits Vanderbilt Children's Hospital, draws some 45,000 people to a premiere sporting and social gathering. (615) 322-7450.

Opryland Gospel Jubilee. Held over Memorial Day and Labor Day, this festival brings together more than a dozen gospel groups, including Opryland's own quartet, the Cumberland Boys, to mark the beginning and end of summer. (615) 889-6611.

Sara Lee Classic LPGA Golf Tournament. This professional golfing event, held the first week in May, features more than 100 of the top women players in the world at the Hermitage Golf Course in Old Hickory, Tennessee. (615) 847-5017.

Tennessee Crafts Fair. For a quarter century, Centennial Park has come alive with the creative wares of craftspeople from across the state the first weekend in May. There is also entertainment, food, demonstrations, and children's craft activities. Sponsored by the Tennessee Association of Craft Artists. (615) 665-0502.

JUNE

American Artisan Festival. Craftspeople from 35 states participate in this mid-June event, showcasing ceramics, wood, leather, fiber, glass, and other handmade objects. There is entertainment, food, and a children's art booth set up under the trees at Centennial Park. (615) 298-4691.

Bellevue Center Balloon Classic. All heads turn upward to witness the hot air balloons that fill the air over Edwin Warner Park. Children's activities and musical performances round out the weekend, which benefits the EAR Foundation at Baptist Hospital. (615) 329-7807.

Dancin' in the District. Every Thursday night during the summer months, Riverfront Park comes alive with music from both local talent and bands from across the country. The free street mixer draws folks from all walks of life, who come to enjoy alfresco entertainment. (615) 242-5600.

International Country Music Fan Fair. This weeklong festival brings in throngs of folks to see their favorite country music stars, who perform and sign autographs at the Tennessee State Fairgrounds. The Grand Masters Fiddling Championship is also part of the activities. Sponsored by the Country Music Association and the Grand Ole Opry, this event is popular the world over, drawing 25,000 people and selling out fast. (615) 889-7503.

Performing Arts Series. During the summer months, the Metro Parks and Recreation department presents a series of free concerts plus dance and theater performances at various parks around the city. (615) 862-8424.

Senior PGA Tour. Well-known professionals descend on Music City to play golf at Opryland's Springhouse Golf Club. Pros like Arnold Palmer, Lee Trevino, and Jack Nicklaus participate in the weeklong event. (615) 871-7759.

Summer Lights in Music City. This is the city's largest outdoor festival, combining music, art, dance, and theater. Music lovers can see a wide variety of entertainment during the four-day downtown event, including some of the city's more well-known stars. The children's arts arcade provides hands-on opportunities, and there are indoor theater productions as well. (615) 726-1875.

JULY

Bobby Jones Gospel Explosion. (See listing in February.)

Dancin' in the District. (See listing in June.)

Independence Day Celebration. Here the flags are unfurled and the fireworks explode to celebrate our country's birthday. Riverfront Park attracts 100,000 revelers for the music and dancing that takes place. (615) 862-8400.

Opryland USA Clogging Championship. Fourteen different categories of competition feature teams, solos, and duets kicking up their heels at this four-day event. (615) 889-6611.

Performing Arts Series. (See listing in June.)

AUGUST

Annual Americana Summer Sampler Craft, Folk Art, and Antique Fair. Dealers from 25 states bring their country crafts, folk art, and antiques to the Tennessee State Fairgrounds for three days of wheeling and dealing. There are also lectures, exhibits, and demonstrations on tap. (615) 227-2080.

Dancin' in the District. (See listing in June.)

Miss Martha's Old Fashioned Ice Cream Crankin'. The shaded lawn of Trinity Presbyterian Church is the site for this annual ice cream festival, where you can sample dozens of homemade varieties that are cranked out fresh. This is a family event, benefiting the Martha O'Bryan Center, complete with children's races and music. (615) 254-1791.

Nashville Shakespeare Festival. The Centennial Park band shell is the site for the free annual production of a Shakespeare play, presented under the evening stars by the Metro Board of Parks and Recreation on weekends during August. (615) 862-8400.

Performing Arts Series. (See listing in June.)

SEPTEMBER

Annual African Street Festival. During this ethnic extravaganza at Tennessee State University, more than 100 merchants from 25 states, poetry, rap, blues, jazz, gospel, R&B, and drama are featured as well as lectures, storytelling, and interesting food. (615) 254-0970.

Belle Meade Fall Fest. The grounds of the Belle Meade Plantation become the backdrop for crafts, antiques, food, and merchandise from local retailers. Music and children's activities add to the fun. (615) 356-0501.

Country Fair. Early 19th-century Middle Tennessee comes alive on the grounds of Travellers Rest with demonstrations of traditional crafts, period music, storytelling, and children's games, plus a bustling marketplace. (615) 832-2962.

Fall Crafts Fair. This juried market of fine crafts showcases artisans from around the country, selected for the quality of their work. Captivating craft demonstrations, food, and entertainment add to the festival fun. Sponsored by the Tennessee Association of Craft Artists and held at Centennial Park. (615) 665-0502.

Home Decorating & Remodeling Show. More than 600 booths of home decorating ideas can provide inspiration if you're in the market to build, remodel, or redecorate. And many items can be bought right off the floor of the Nashville Convention Center during the four-day show. (615) 748-9980.

Italian Street Fair. This benefit for the Nashville Symphony Orchestra offers Italian sausage sandwiches, carnival rides, entertainment, and arts and crafts. You may even see a game of *bocce* ball at this festival, which takes place at Riverfront Park in downtown Nashville. (615) 329-3033.

Music City Blues Festival. Nashville pays tribute to blues legend B.B. King with a birthday party at Riverfront Park that features the king himself as well as well-known blues singers like Etta James, Jimmie Vaughan, and Elvin Bishop. (615) 320-9333.

Opryland Gospel Jubilee. (See listing in May.)

Tennessee State Fair. The midway brings in families for the rides and maybe the cotton candy, but the fair is a huge livestock and agricultural competition, with 4-H Club kids strutting their stuff. You'll also find crafts, antiques, and food products up for grabs. Held, of course, at the Tennessee State Fairgrounds. (615) 862-8980.

OCTOBER

Grand Ole Opry Birthday. More than 20,000 Opry fans take part in a birthday bash each October. The three-day celebration gives music lovers a chance to see concerts and a Grand Ole Opry performance, plus get their favorite stars' autographs and pictures. (615) 889-6611.

Music & Molasses Festival. The grounds of the Ellington Agricultural Center come alive during mid-October for this festival that showcases Tennessee crafts, music, fiddling, pumpkins, cloggers, demonstrations, storytelling, and molasses making. (615) 360-0197.

NAIA Pow Wow. Native Americans from the United States and Canada gather for three days of dancing, arts and crafts, storytelling, and demonstrations. Food booths offer traditional fare from different tribes at this annual celebration, which usually takes place at Hermitage Landing. (615) 726-0806.

Oktoberfest. Historic Germantown celebrates its heritage with authentic German food, entertainment, polka dancing, and both German and American crafts. A special worship service kicks off the festivities at Church of the Assumption Catholic church and the Monroe Street United Methodist Church, sponsors of the one-day event. (615) 256-2729.

Southern Festival of Books. Literary types won't want to miss the panel discussions, book signings, sales, and readings with authors from across the United States, particularly the Southeast. The three-day event, held at Legislative Plaza, is sponsored by the Tennessee Humanities Council and is nationally recognized. (615) 320-7001.

Storytelling Festival. Several different locations at The Hermitage provide the backdrop for storytellers at this three-day event. The focus is on American and Tennessee folktales of the 19th century, and the festival features both local and nationally known storytellers. (615) 889-2941.

NOVEMBER

Annual Americana Christmas Sampler Craft, Folk Art, and Antique Fair. In early November you can start your holiday shopping at this craft fair, held at the Tennessee State Fairgrounds and featuring 200 dealers from 25 states. (615) 227-2080.

Christmas at Belle Meade Plantation. The Belle Meade Mansion gets decked out for a Victorian Christmas, with costumed interpreters explaining about customs and traditions of the 19th century. Traditional Christmas dinners served in the 1872 carriage house and special candlelight tours are scheduled for the season. (615) 356-0501.

Christmas Village. Here's another three-day shopping opportunity, with more than 250 craftspeople and merchants selling seasonal gift items. Clothing, wreaths, jewelry, baskets, and other objects await shoppers, and children can enjoy a visit with Santa. This event benefits the Bill Wilkerson Hearing and Speech Center. (615) 320-5353.

A Country Christmas/Christmas at Opryland. From November 1 through Christmas Day, the Opryland Hotel offers a plethora of activities, including musical stage shows, craft fairs, international Christmas dinners, and a Yule log lighting ceremony. The Opryland theme park is lit up from mid-November through the end of December, and there is special entertainment, holiday food, and what's said to be the nation's largest nativity scene. (615) 889-6611.

Sinking Creek Film/Video Festival. This weeklong festival honors the best in independently produced films and videos. Sinking Creek, which is held on the Vanderbilt University campus, is the oldest film festival in the South and the only one in Tennessee. The workshops, seminars, and screenings attract people from all over the country. (615) 322-4234.

DECEMBER

Christmas Parade and Rudolph's Red Nose Run. More than 100 floats, bands, clowns, and even Santa await parade-goers for this annual commemoration of the holiday. A 5K race and a mile-long fun run take place first, with prizes awarded for best costumes and time. Sponsored by Nashville Gas. (615) 734-1754.

Trees of Christmas. Fifteen large trees all trimmed with a different theme decorate Cheekwood's Botanic Hall in a display that has become a Nashville tradition for more than 30 years. The spectacle is especially fun for children. (615) 353-2150.

Twelfth Night Celebration. During weekends in December, Travellers Rest welcomes guests to an authentic Twelfth Night celebration with candlelight tours, food, and holiday music. (615) 832-8197.

INDEX

This index lists places and organizations that might help you get your bearings if you're new to Nashville or are visiting for a short time. Due to their changing nature, clubs and restaurants, retail establishments, and hotel accommodations have not been included here.

ABOUT THE AUTHOR

Susan Chappell has been a book, magazine, and newspaper editor and writer since 1980. She was the assistant lifestyles editor and restaurant critic for the *Nashville Banner* and continues to cover visual arts for the newspaper. Her articles have appeared in magazines such as *Parenting, Nashville, Southpoint,* and *St. Louis.*

Susan is the senior editor for food and travel for *Nashville Life* magazine and writes restaurant reviews and stories about day-trip travel for the city magazine. She is also the author of *Day Trips From Nashville,* published by Two Lane Press of Kansas City, which is a guide to places to go within a couple hours' drive of the city. Susan lives in Nashville with her husband and two children.